# SRA Reading Mastery

CLASSIC EDITION

## Seatwork
## Blackline Master Book

## Level I

**Siegfried Engelmann**
**Elaine C. Bruner**

A Division of The McGraw·Hill Companies

Columbus, Ohio

**Lessons with cutouts**
3, 6, 7, 9, 11, 14, 16, 25, 29, 33, 37, 46, 48, 49, 50, 51, 52, 54, 56, 58, 64, 66, 72, 79, 81, 86, 88, 102, 112, 121, 125, 136, 143, 147, 148, 152, 156, 160

**Note to the Teacher**
The activities in this book will reinforce the materials presented in the *Reading Mastery* Classic Edition, Level I program. They correlate with *Reading Mastery* in their orthography, vocabulary, and skill development. If you are using the *Reading Mastery: Fast Cycle* program, a lesson conversion chart appears on the last page of this book.

Each activity focuses on a major reading skill in one of the following categories: sound discrimination, word recognition, sentence structure, literal comprehension, following directions, sequencing, inferential comprehension, and paraphrasing. The skill is identified at the bottom of each page.

The directions at the top of each page are to be read to the students. Most children will be able to work the activities without further help, but some children will need more guidance. You may want to expand on the directions and perhaps even "walk through" each new type of activity with your students the first time it appears. If your students appear to be having difficulty with a particular activity, just skip those activities for a while. You may want to try them again later, when you think your children are ready for them.

**School Use of Blackline Masters**
Use the blackline masters in this book for making duplicating masters or for photocopying. They may be reproduced for classroom use by schools without the prior written permission of SRA.

**Do not** reproduce a lesson on the reverse side of a lesson that has cutouts.

www.sra4kids.com

**SRA/McGraw-Hill**
*A Division of The McGraw-Hill Companies*

Send all inquiries to:
SRA/McGraw-Hill
8787 Orion Place
Columbus, OH 43240-4027

Printed in the United States of America.

ISBN 0-07-569272-4

1 2 3 4 5 6 7 8 9 MAL 06 05 04 03 02

Name _____     **Lesson 1**

*(Point to the star in the upper left corner.)* This is a star. Put a red mark on it.
Find the other stars in this picture and color them red.

**Decoding Readiness**     Reading Mastery I Seatwork

Parts of this picture are missing. Find the part of the dog that's missing. Follow the dots with your pencil. Then fix up the door and the tree.

**Decoding Readiness**    **Reading Mastery I Seatwork**

Cut out the trees at the bottom of the page.  Cut along the dotted lines.  Paste each tree next to the one that looks just like it.  Then color all the trees.

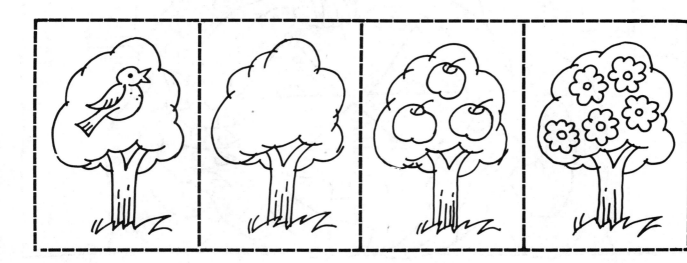

**Decoding Readiness**     **Reading Mastery I Seatwork**

*(Point to the triangle in the upper left corner.)* This is a triangle. Put a red mark on it.
Find the other triangles in this picture and color them red.

**Decoding Readiness**    **Reading Mastery I Seatwork**

Parts of this picture are missing. Find the part of the flower that's missing. Follow the dots with your pencil. Then fix up the shoe and the bench leg.

**Decoding Readiness**    Reading Mastery I Seatwork

Cut out the kites at the bottom of the page. Cut along the dotted lines. Paste each kite next to the one that looks just like it. Then color all the kites.

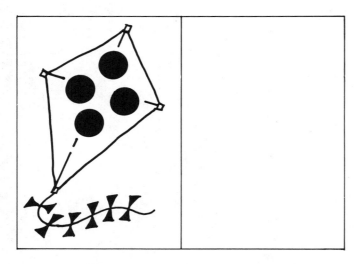

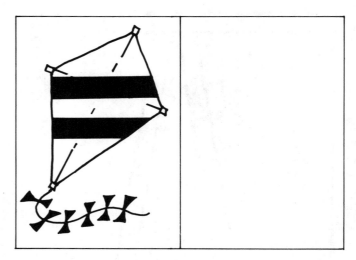

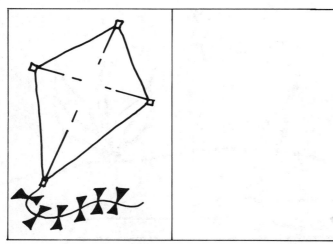

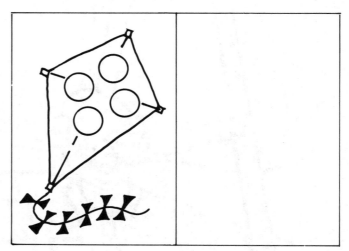

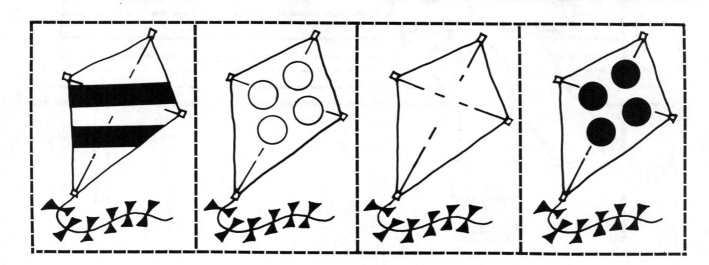

Cut out the pictures at the bottom of the page. Cut along the dotted lines. Paste each picture under the one that is just like it. Then color all the pictures.

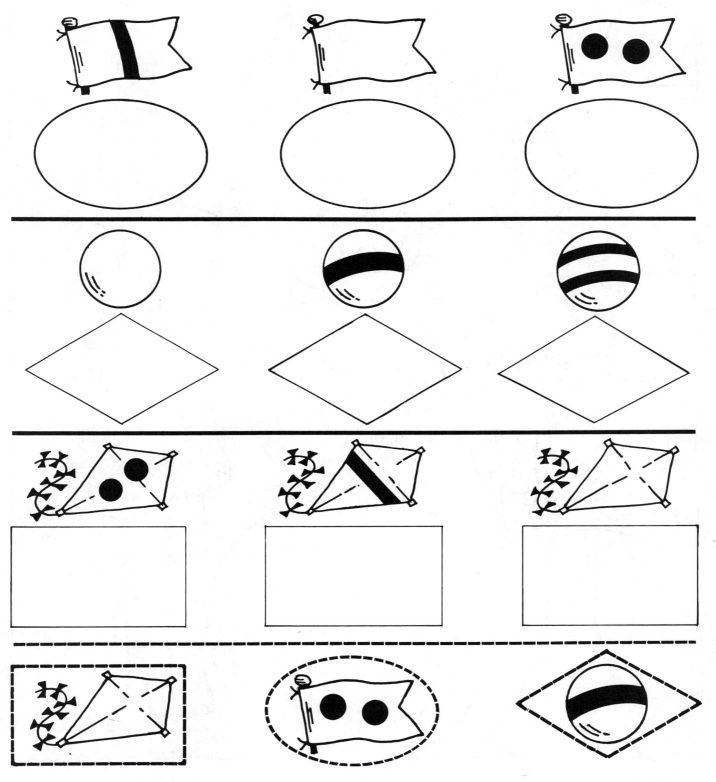

**Decoding Readiness     Reading Mastery I Seatwork**

Name _____ **Lesson 8**

*(Point to the circle in the upper left corner.)* This is a circle. Put a red mark on it.
Find the other circles in this picture and color them red.

**Decoding Readiness**   Reading Mastery I Seatwork

**Name** _____

Cut out the pictures at the bottom of the page.  Cut along the dotted lines.  Paste each picture under the one that is just like it.  Then color all the pictures.

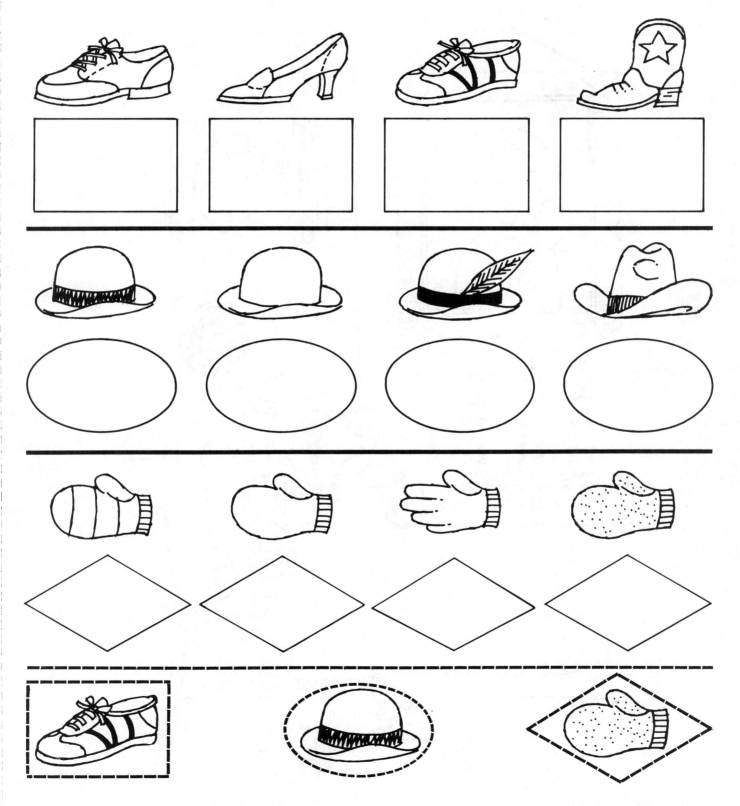

Parts of this picture are missing. Find the part of the cup that's missing. Follow the dots with your pencil. Then fix up the candle and the picture frame.

**Decoding Readiness**   Reading Mastery I Seatwork

Cut out the pictures at the bottom of the page. Cut along the dotted lines. Paste each picture under the one that is just like it. Then color all the pictures.

**Decoding Readiness** **Reading Mastery I Seatwork**

First trace the *mmm's* on the page. Then start with the big dot and follow the dotted line around. You'll make a picture of something that monkeys like to play in. Color the picture that you make.

Help the alligator get to the river.  Start with the alligator at the top of the puzzle and draw a line from *aaa* to *aaa* until you reach the river.  When you finish, fill in the row of *aaa*'s at the bottom of the page.

**Sounds and Letters**   Reading Mastery I Seatwork

Trace the sounds at the bottom of the page. Then cut them out. Cut along the dotted lines. Paste the sounds on the matching sounds in the picture. When you finish, color the picture.

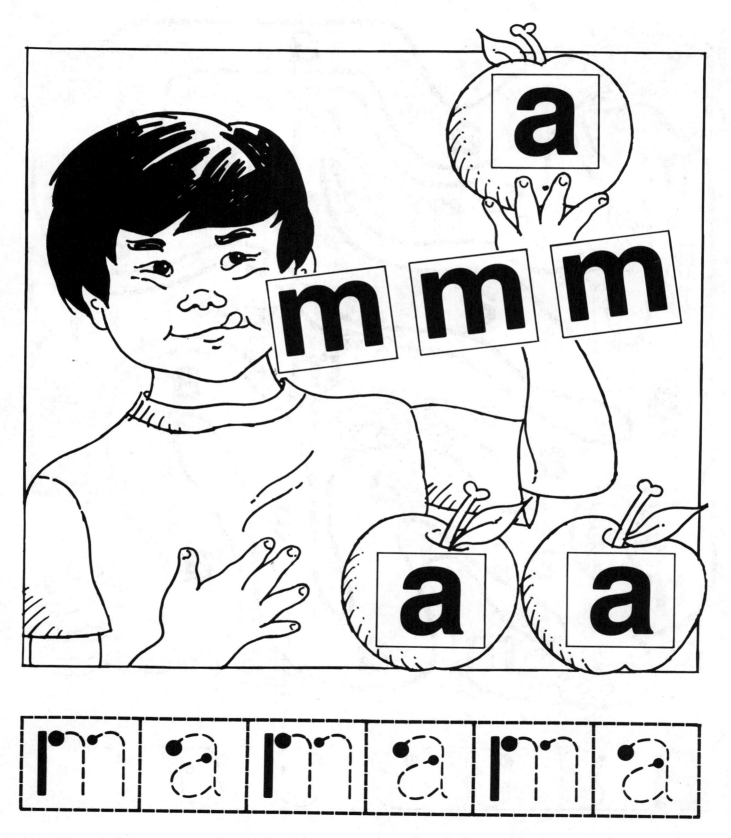

**Sounds and Letters**   **Reading Mastery I Seatwork**

In each row, circle the picture that goes with the thing in the box. When you finish all the rows, trace something that goes with the dog at the bottom of the page. Color your picture.

**Comprehension Readiness     Reading Mastery I Seatwork**

Trace the sounds at the bottom of the page. Then cut them out. Cut along the dotted lines. Paste the sounds on the matching sounds in the picture. When you finish, color the picture.

**Sounds and Letters** Reading Mastery I Seatwork

First trace the *sss's* on the page. Then start with the big dot and follow the dotted line around. You'll make a picture of a big sailboat. Color the picture that you make.

There's a picture hidden on this page.  To find the hidden picture, color all the shapes that have *sss* in them brown.

**Sounds and Letters**     Reading Mastery I Seatwork

In each row, circle the picture that goes with the thing in the box. When you finish all the rows, trace something that goes with the monkey at the bottom of the page. Color your picture.

Comprehension Readiness  Reading Mastery I Seatwork

Help the eagle get to its nest. Start with the eagle at the bottom of the puzzle and draw a line from ēēē to ēēē until you reach the nest. When you finish, fill in the row of ēēē's at the bottom of the page.

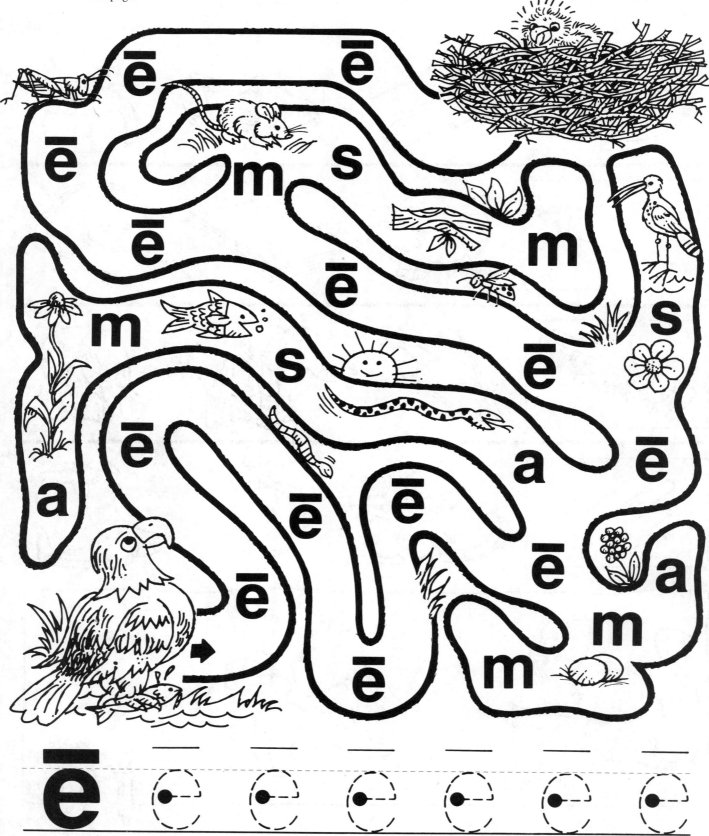

There's a picture hidden on this page. To find the hidden picture, color all the shapes that have ēēē in them black.

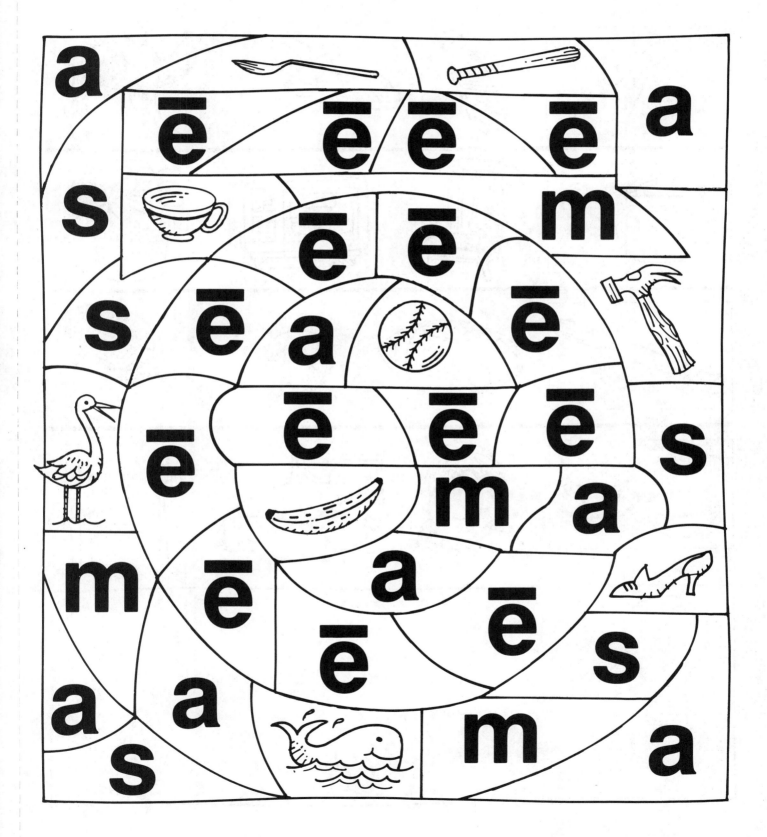

**Sounds and Letters**    **Reading Mastery I Seatwork**

In each row, circle the picture that goes with the thing in the box. When you finish all the rows, trace something that goes with the light bulb at the bottom of the page. Color your picture.

**Comprehension Readiness** Reading Mastery I Seatwork

One of the pictures in each row is in a box. One of the other pictures shows what happened just before the picture in the box. Circle the 3 pictures that show what happened just before.

**Comprehension Readiness**     **Reading Mastery I Seatwork**

Help the rocketship get to the moon.  Start with the rocketship and draw a line from *rrr* to *rrr* until you reach the moon.  When you finish, fill in the row of *rrr*'s at the bottom of the page.

r r r r r

r r r r

r m a a

r r r r m r

r r r r s

m r r r r

r e

r r s r a

r m r r r a r

r _ _ _ _ _ _

**Sounds and Letters**   Reading Mastery I Seatwork

There's an animal hidden on this page.  To find the animal, cut out the boxes at the bottom of the page.
Cut along the dotted lines.  Paste each box on the one that has the same sound in it.  Color the animal
that you find.

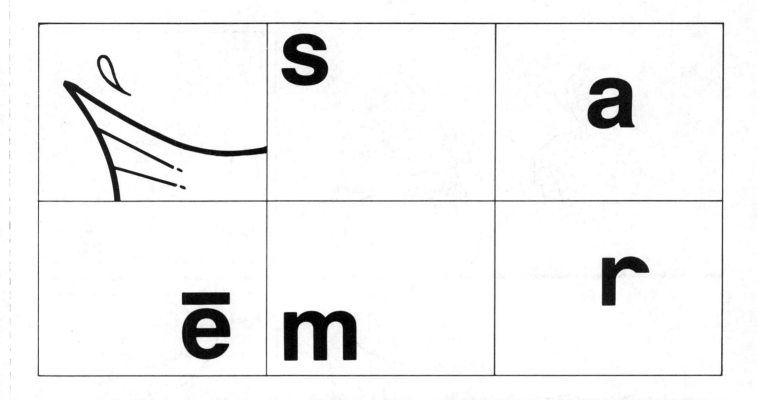

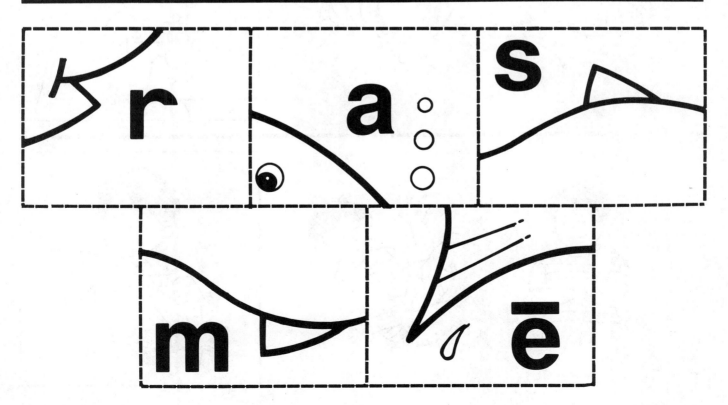

**Sounds and Letters**     Reading Mastery I Seatwork

One of the pictures in each row is in a box. One of the other pictures shows what happened just before the picture in the box. Circle the 3 pictures that show what happened just before.

**Comprehension Readiness**  Reading Mastery I Seatwork

**Name** _____ **Lesson 27**

In each row, circle the picture that goes with the thing in the box. When you finish all the rows, trace something that goes with the nest at the bottom of the page. Color your picture.

**Comprehension Readiness**  Reading Mastery I Seatwork

(*Point to* d *in upper right corner.*) Put a red mark on this *d.*
Find the other *d's* in this picture. Trace each *d* with red. Then color the rest of the picture.

**Sounds and Letters**   **Reading Mastery I Seatwork**

There's an animal hidden on this page. To find the animal, cut out the boxes at the bottom of the page. Cut along the dotted lines. Paste each box on the one that has the same sound in it. Color the animal that you find.

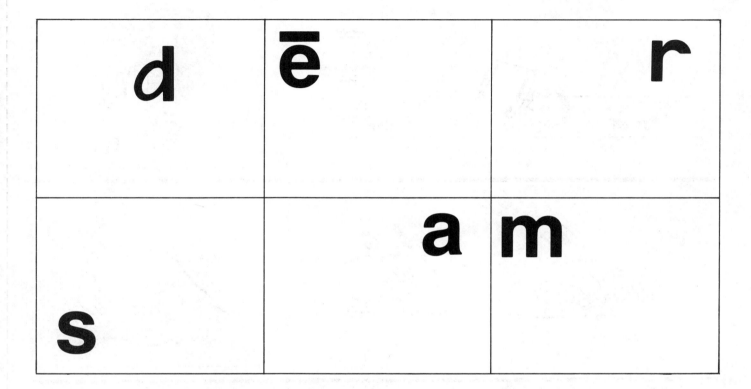

**Sounds and Letters**    Reading Mastery I Seatwork

Name _____ **Lesson 30**

One of the pictures in each row is in a box. One of the other pictures shows what happened just before the picture in the box. Circle the 4 pictures that show what happened just before.

  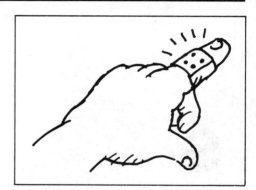

**Comprehension Readiness**     Reading Mastery I Seatwork

There's a picture hidden on this page.  To find the hidden picture, color all the shapes that have *d* in them green.

**Sounds and Letters**   Reading Mastery I Seatwork

Help the foot get to the shoe. Start with the foot at the top of the puzzle and draw a line from *fff* to *fff* until you reach the shoe. When you finish, fill in the row of *fff*'s at the bottom of the page.

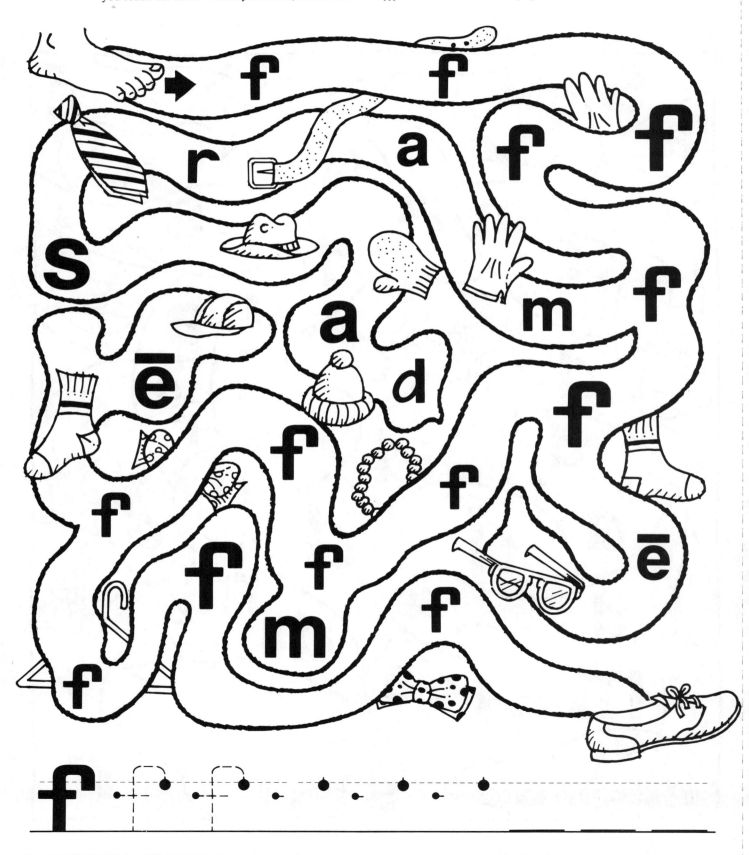

There's an animal hidden on this page. To find the animal, cut out the boxes at the bottom of the page. Cut along the dotted lines. Paste each box on the one that has the same word in it. Color the animal that you find.

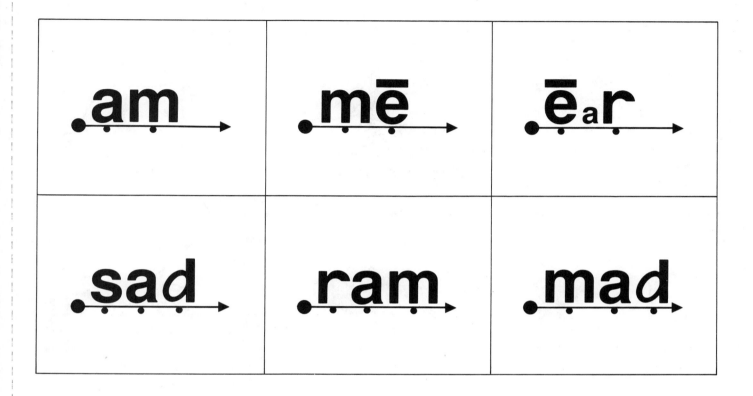

One of the pictures in each row is in a box. One of the other pictures shows what happened just before the picture in the box. Circle the 4 pictures that show what happened just before.

**Comprehension Readiness   Reading Mastery I Seatwork**

There's a picture hidden on this page.  To find the hidden picture, color all the shapes that have *iii* in them orange.

The pictures may not show what happened first and what happened next. The numbers are already written for the first two rows. In each row, put a *1* by the picture that happened *first* and a *2* by the picture that happened *next*. When you finish the page, go back and color the pictures.

Comprehension Readiness    Reading Mastery I Seatwork

There's an animal hidden on this page. To find the animal, cut out the boxes at the bottom of the page. Cut along the dotted lines. Paste each box on the one that has the same word in it. Color the animal that you find.

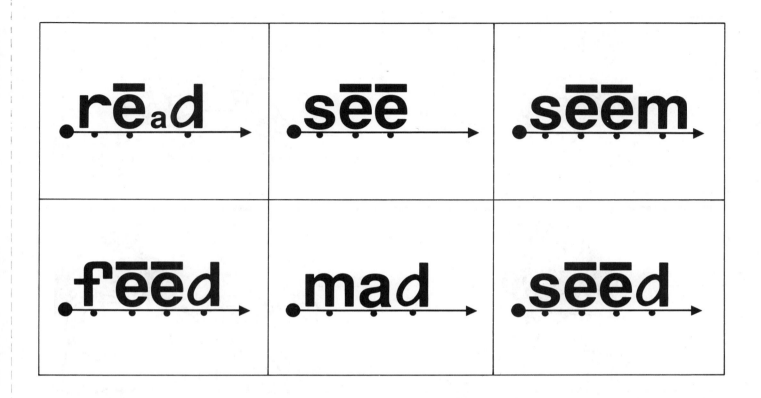

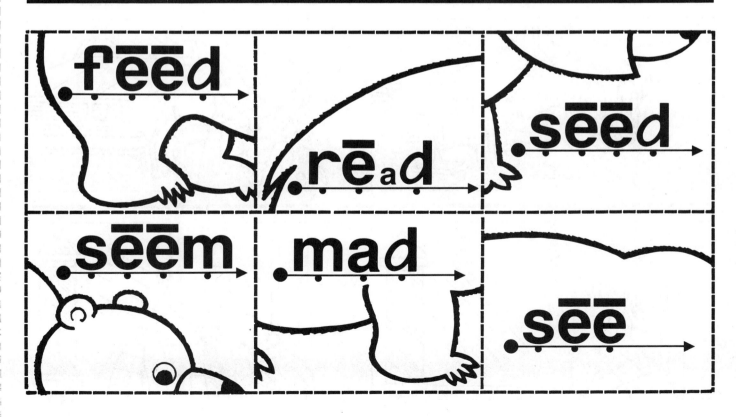

Words    Reading Mastery I Seatwork

The pictures may not show what happened first and what happened next. In each row, put a *1* by the picture that happened *first* and a *2* by the picture that happened *next*. When you finish the page, go back and color the pictures.

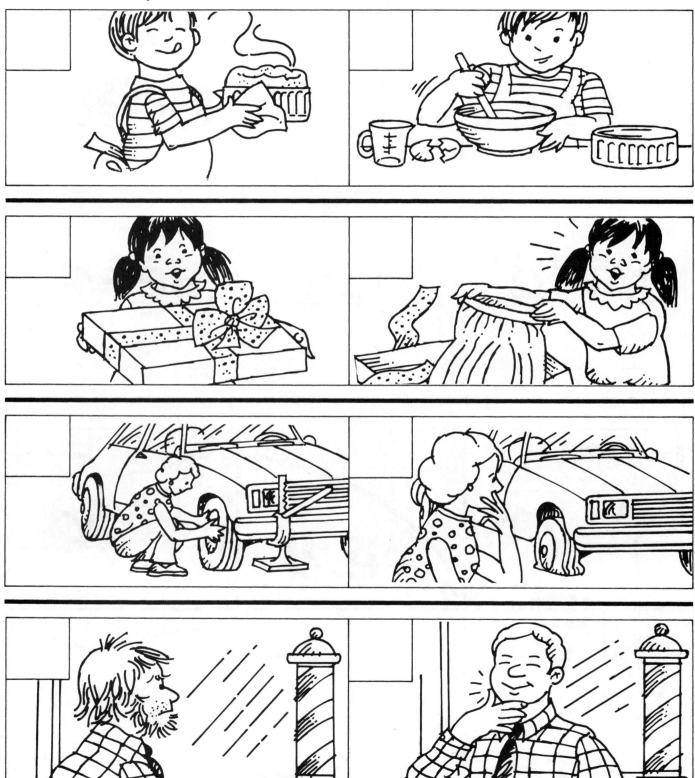

**Comprehension Readiness**     Reading Mastery I Seatwork

(*Point to* th *in upper left corner.*) Put a red mark on this *th*. Find the other *ththth*'s in this picture. Trace each *ththth* with red. Then color the rest of the picture.

**Sounds and Letters**   Reading Mastery I Seatwork

Write the words on the page. First trace each word. Then copy the word. When you finish, draw a picture of somebody saying *me*.

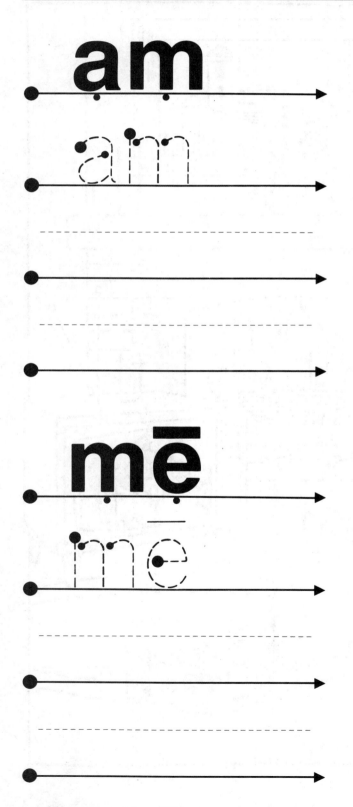

Words   Reading Mastery I Seatwork

The pictures may not show what happened first and what happened next. In each row, put a *1* by the picture that happened *first* and a *2* by the picture that happened *next*. When you finish the page, go back and color the pictures.

The pictures do not show what happened first, what happened next, and what happened last in order. In each row, put a *1* by the picture that happened *first,* a *2* by the picture that happened *next,* and a *3* by the picture that happened *last.* When you finish the page, go back and color the pictures.

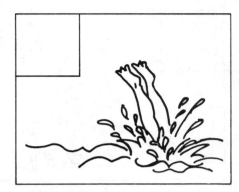

**Comprehension Readiness**     **Reading Mastery I Seatwork**

The pictures do not show what happened first, what happened next, and what happened last in order. In each row, put a *1* by the picture that happened *first,* a *2* by the picture that happened *next,* and a *3* by the picture that happened *last.* When you finish the page, go back and color the pictures.

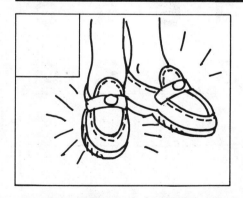  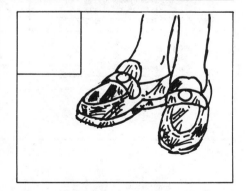

**Comprehension Readiness**   **Reading Mastery I Seatwork**

Name _____ **Lesson 44**

Read the word on the arrow at the beginning of each row of letters. That word is hidden in the row of letters. Find the hidden words and circle them. The first row is already done. After you find the hidden words, complete the picture of an animal that is *sad*.

| feed | f | d | (f | ē | ē | d) | ē | f |
|------|---|---|----|---|---|----|---|---|
| mad | a | m | d | m | d | m | a | d |
| mē | ē | m | m | ē | ē | ē | m | m |
| ram | m | r | a | r | a | m | m | a |
| am | m | m | a | a | a | m | m | a |
| sēē | ē | ē | s | ē | s | ē | ē | s |
| sēēd | d | s | ē | ē | d | ē | s | ē |
| sad | s | a | d | d | s | a | a | d |

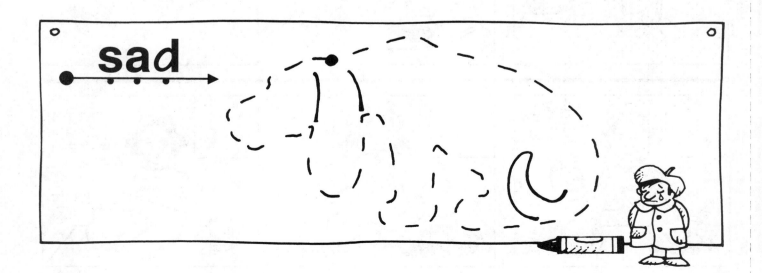

sad

Copyright © by SRA/McGraw-Hill. Permission is granted to reproduce this page for classroom use.

**Words    Reading Mastery I Seatwork**

The pictures do not show what happened first, what happened next, and what happened last in order. In each row, put a *1* by the picture that happened *first,* a *2* by the picture that happened *next,* and a *3* by the picture that happened *last.* When you finish the page, go back and color the pictures.

**Comprehension Readiness** Reading Mastery I Seatwork

Make two picture stories on this page.  Cut out the pictures at the bottom of the page.  Paste each set of pictures in the right order so they tell a story.

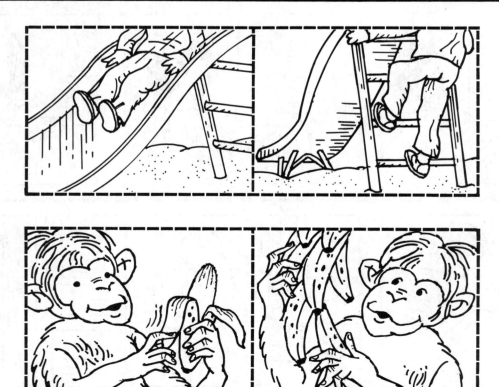

**Comprehension Readiness**     **Reading Mastery I Seatwork**

Write the words on the page. First trace each word. Then copy the word. When you finish, draw a picture of somebody who is *mad*.

**Words**    **Reading Mastery I Seatwork**

There's an animal hidden on this page. To find the animal, cut out the boxes at the bottom of the page. Cut along the dotted lines. Paste each box on the one that has the same word in it. Color the animal that you find.

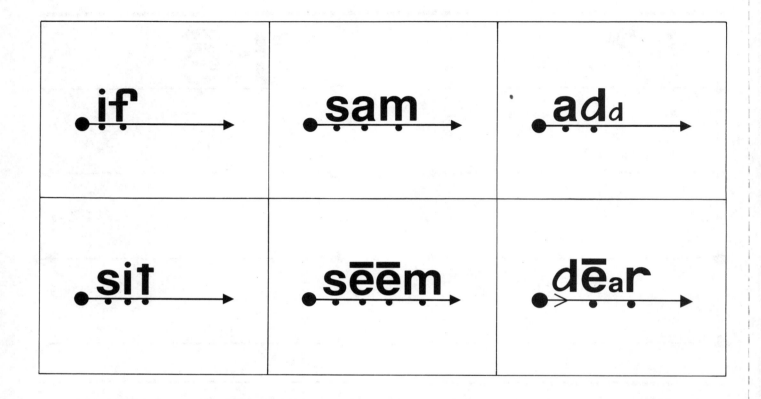

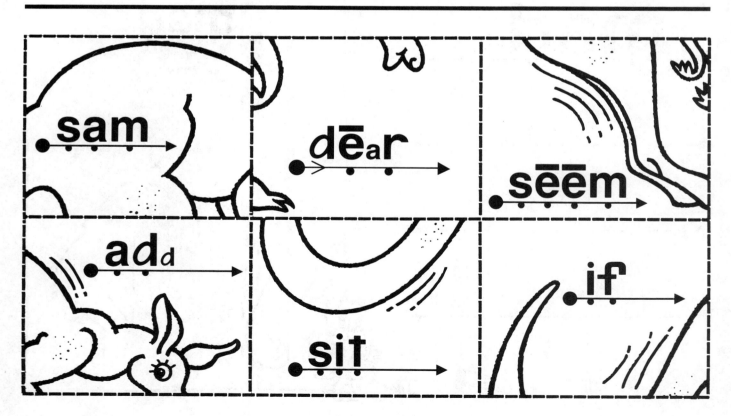

Make two picture stories on this page.  Cut out the pictures at the bottom of the page.  Paste each set of pictures in the right order so they tell a story.

**Comprehension Readiness**     Reading Mastery I Seatwork

Cut out the words at the bottom of the page. Paste them on the worm parts so the words
make sentences. When you finish, turn your paper over and draw a picture of one of your sentences.

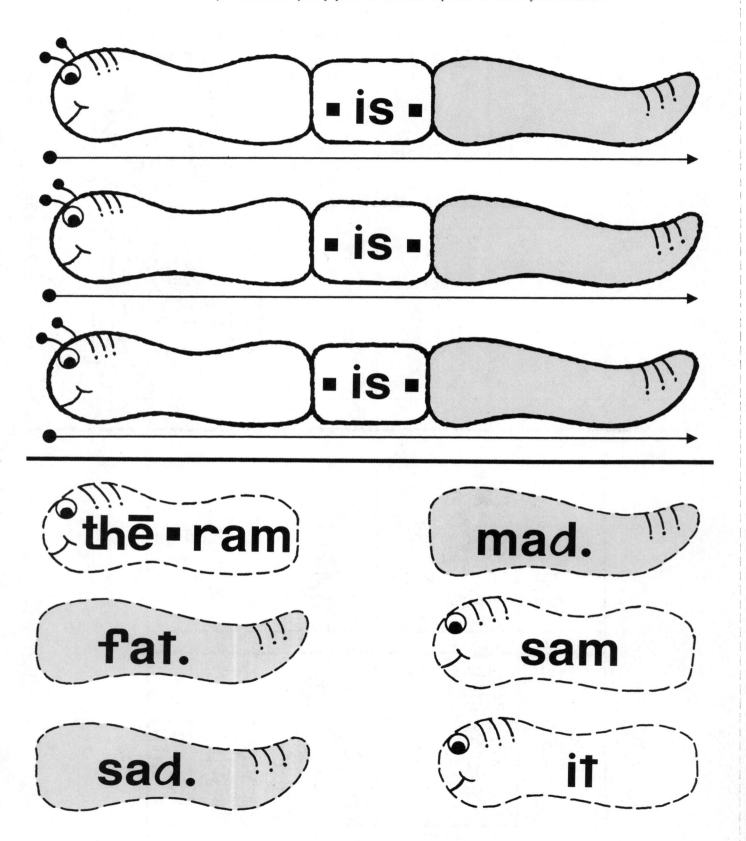

Sentences    Reading Mastery I Seatwork

Name_____ **Lesson 51**

Copy the sound *t* in each box at the bottom of the page. Then cut out the boxes that have *t*.
Paste one under each picture that shows a word that begins with *t*.

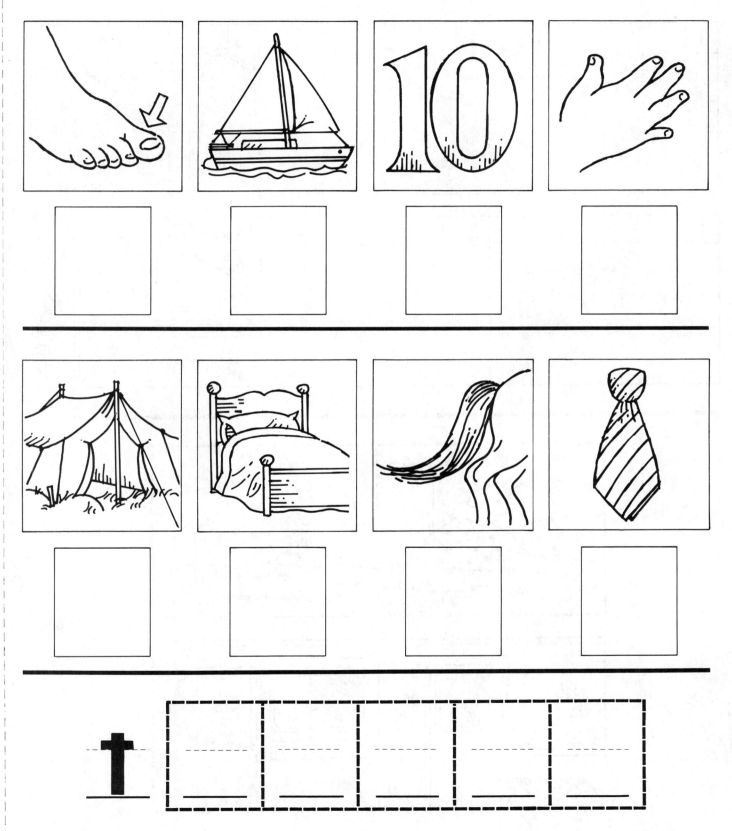

Make two picture stories on this page.  Cut out the pictures at the bottom of the page.  Paste each set of pictures in the right order so they tell a story.

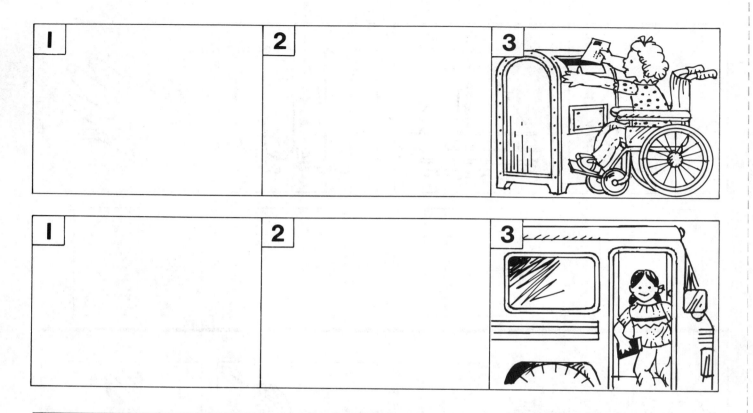

Comprehension Readiness     Reading Mastery I Seatwork

Choose the right arrow for each picture. Copy the words on the bottom arrow. When you finish, color the pictures.

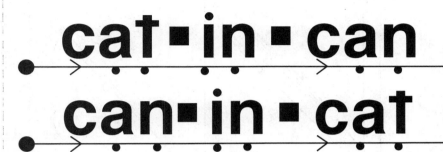

## cat ▪ in ▪ can

## can ▪ in ▪ cat

▪          ▪

## man ▪ on ▪ ram

## ram ▪ on ▪ man

▪          ▪

## sam ▪ in ▪ sēēd

## sēēd ▪ in ▪ sam

▪          ▪

**Literal Comprehension**   Reading Mastery I Seatwork

Copy the sound *nnn* in each box at the bottom of the page. Then cut out the boxes that have *nnn*.
Paste one under each picture that shows a word that begins with *nnn*.

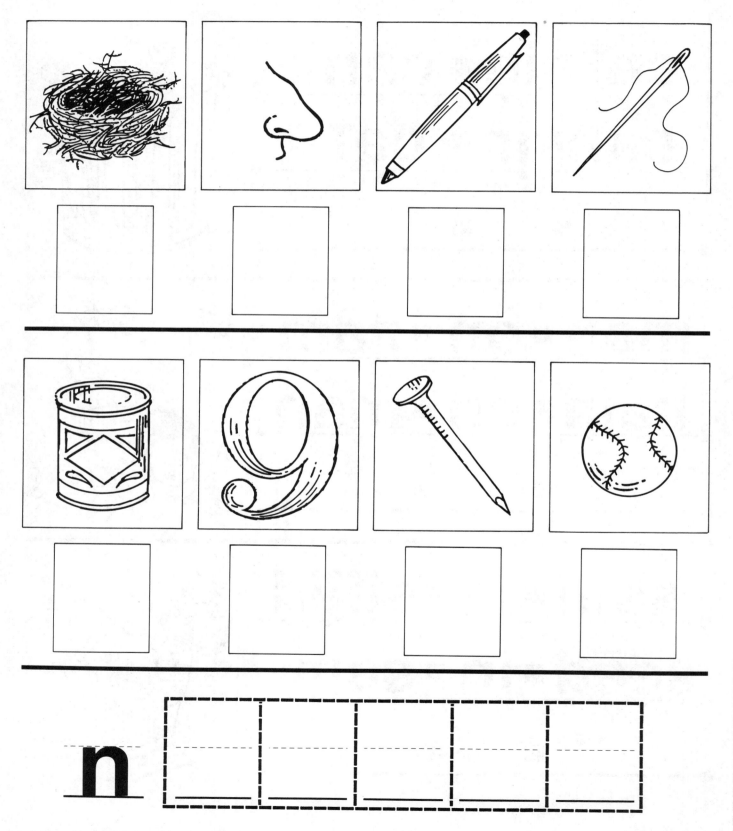

n

Read the word on the arrow at the beginning of each row of letters. That word is hidden in the row of letters. Find the hidden words and circle them. The first row is already done. After you find the hidden words, complete the picture of the last word—*Sam.*

| dim → | (d i m) i d d m d |
|---|---|
| mad → | a a m a d d m a |
| miss → | s s i s m i s s |
| sēēm → | m m s ē ē m s ē |
| sit → | t i s t i s i t |
| at → | t a a t t a a a |
| sēē → | ē s ē ē s s s ē |
| sam → | a s m m s a m m |

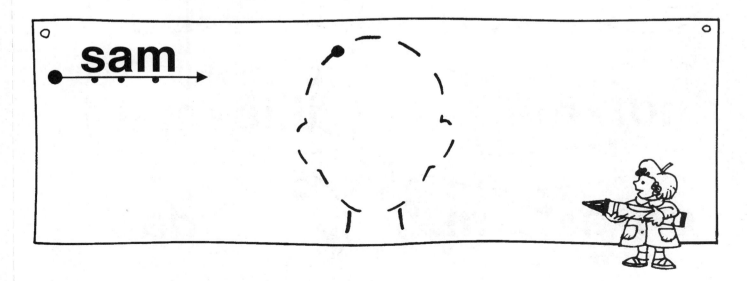

sam →

**Words**     Reading Mastery I Seatwork

Cut out the words at the bottom of the page. Paste them on the worm parts so the words make sentences. When you finish, turn your paper over and draw a picture of one of your sentences.

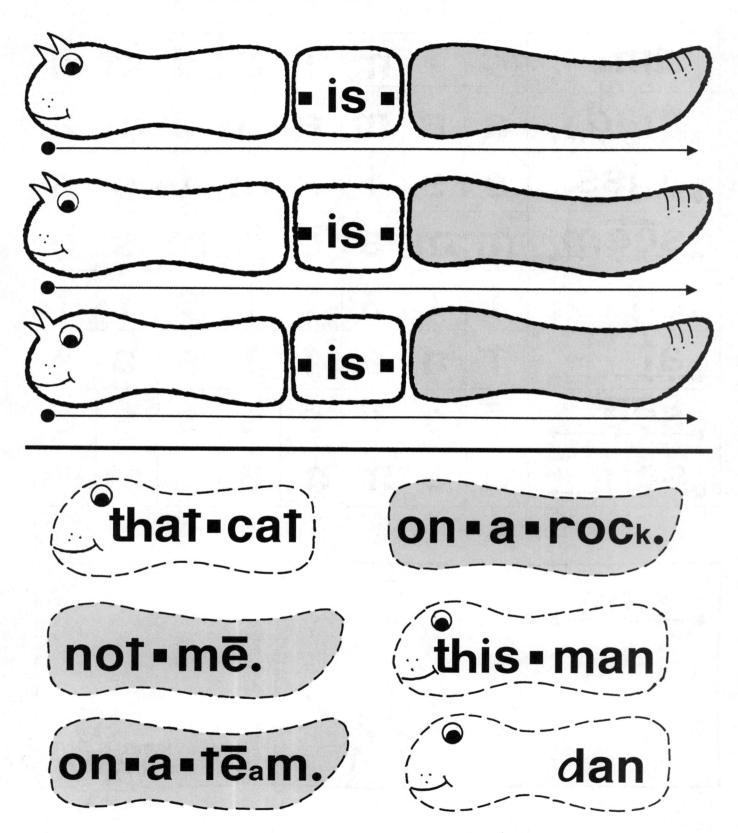

Copy each sentence next to the picture it matches.  Then color the pictures.

dan ∎ is ∎ sad.

dan ∎ is ∎ mad.

dan ∎ is ∎ tan.

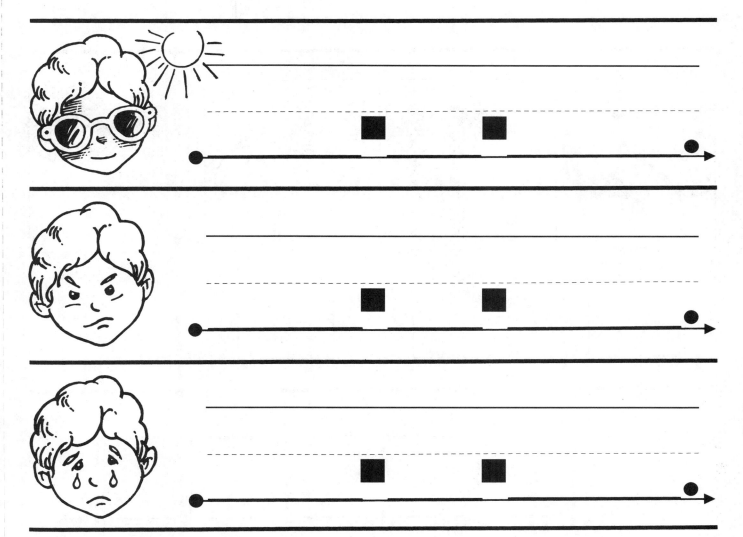

Copy the sound *c* in each box at the bottom of the page. Then cut out the boxes that have *c*.
Paste one under each picture that shows a word that begins with *c*.

**Sounds and Letters**   Reading Mastery I Seatwork

Write the sentences on the page. First trace each sentence. Then copy the sentence. When you finish, draw a picture of a *sad cat*.

fēēd ▪ thē ▪ cat.

fēēd ▪ thē ▪ cat.

it ▪ is ▪ sad.

it ▪ is ▪ sad.

sad ▪ cat

Read the word on the arrow at the beginning of each row of letters. That word is hidden in the row of letters. Find the hidden words and circle them. The first row is already done. After you find the hidden words, complete the picture of the last word—*Dan*.

| fin → | f i n | n | f | i | f | n |
|---|---|---|---|---|---|---|
| in → | n i | i | i | n | n i | i |
| tin → | n i | t | n | i | t | i n |
| an → | n | n a | a | a | n | n |
| sit → | t | s i | t | i | s | s t |
| sēēd → | ē | d s | ē | ē | d | s d |
| ran → | a | n n | r | r a | n | n r |
| dan → | n | a d | a | d | d | a n |

| dan → |

Make each word match the picture next to it. Choose the correct sound from the box and write it in the blank.

| s m | r c |
|---|---|
| ṃad | at |
| sad | at |

| f r | m s |
|---|---|
| an | ēₐt |
| an | ēₐt |

| t s | r s |
|---|---|
| acₖ | ocₖ |
| acₖ | ocₖ |

**Words**   Reading Mastery I Seatwork

Choose the right arrow for each picture. Copy the words on the bottom arrow.
When you finish, color the pictures.

dan ▪ on ▪ fēēt

fēēt ▪ on ▪ dan

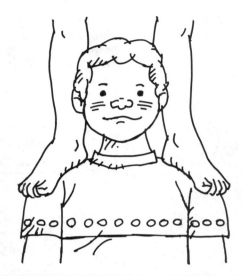

rat ▪ on ▪ cat

cat ▪ on ▪ rat

fin ▪ on ▪ fan

fan ▪ on ▪ fin

**Literal Comprehension** Reading Mastery I Seatwork

Write the sentences on the page. First trace each sentence. Then copy the sentence.
When you finish, draw a picture of a *neat sock*.

# thē ∙ sock ∙ fit.

the ∙ sock ∙ fit.

---

# it ∙ is ∙ nēₐt.

it ∙ is ∙ nēₐt.

nēₐt ∙ sock

Cut out the words at the bottom of the page. Paste them on the worm parts so the words make sentences.
When you finish, turn your paper over and draw a picture of one of your sentences.

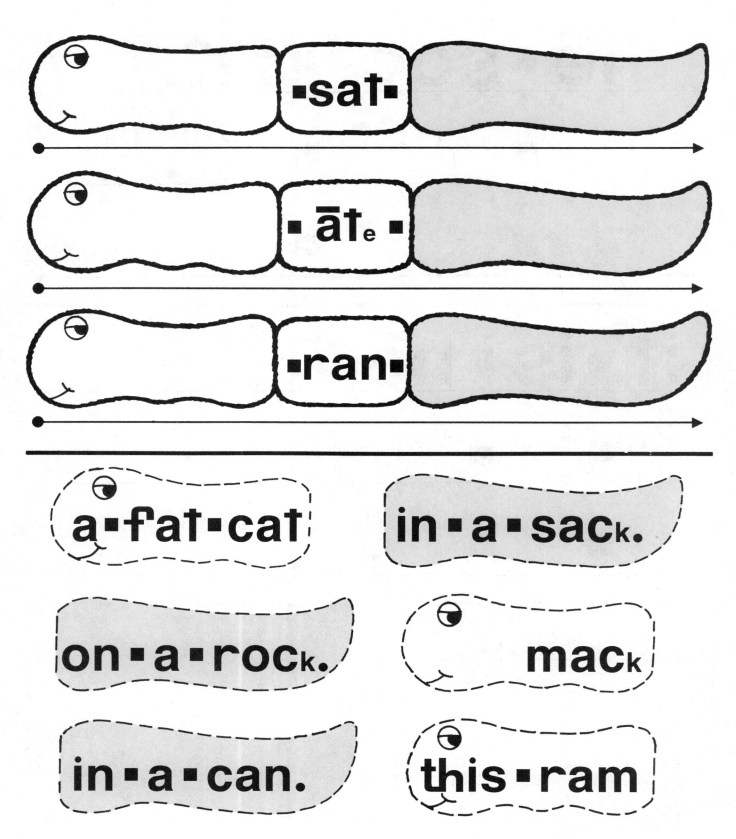

Put the words in order. Write them in the boxes. Then finish the pictures so they show what the words say.

**a**

**on**

**cat**

| o | n | ■ | a | ■ | c | a | t |

**in**

**can**

**a**

| | | ■ | | ■ | | | |

**man**

**on**

**a**

| | | ■ | | ■ | | | |

**Literal Comprehension**  Reading Mastery I Seatwork

Cut out the words at the bottom of the page.  Paste each word in the box next to the picture it matches.
Then copy the words.

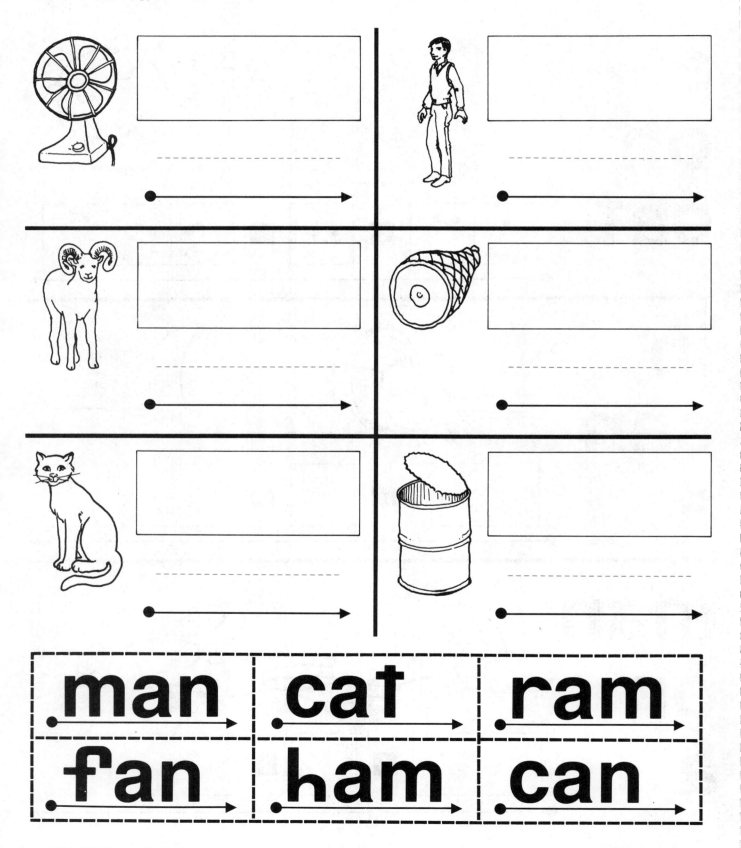

Copy each sentence next to the picture it matches.  Then color the pictures.

# thē ▪ cat ▪ sat.
# thē ▪ cat ▪ ran.
# thē ▪ cat ▪ fit.

Make each word match the picture next to it. Choose the correct sound from the box and write it in the blank.

| h   r |

\_\_\_\_ **am** →

\_\_\_\_ **am** →

| s   r |

\_\_\_\_ **un** →

\_\_\_\_ **un** →

| s   h |

\_\_\_\_ **it** →

\_\_\_\_ **it** →

| c   m |

\_\_\_\_ **an** →

\_\_\_\_ **an** →

| s   f |

\_\_\_\_ **ēēd** →

\_\_\_\_ **ēēd** →

| t   f |

\_\_\_\_ **ēar** →

\_\_\_\_ **ēar** →

Put the words in order. Write them in the boxes. Then finish the pictures so they show what the words say.

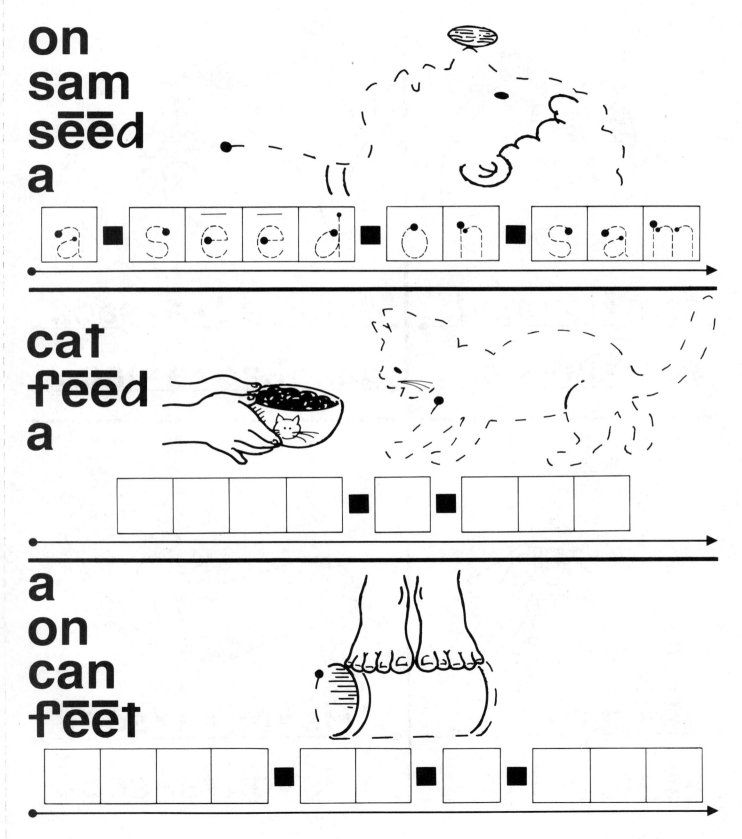

on
sam
sēēd
a

| a | ■ | s | ē | ē | d | ■ | o | n | ■ | s | a | m |

cat
fēēd
a

can
feet
on
a

**Literal Comprehension**     Reading Mastery I Seatwork

Circle the sentence that tells about each picture. When you finish, color all the pictures.

. **sam ▪ is ▪ mad.** →

. **sam ▪ is ▪ sic**k**.** →

. *dan ▪ had ▪ a ▪ sac*k**.** →

. *dan ▪ had ▪ a ▪ tac*k**.** →

. h**ē** ▪ can ▪ roc**k.** →

. h**ē** ▪ can ▪ hit. →

. **it ▪ is ▪ on ▪ a ▪ sē**a**t.** →

. **it ▪ is ▪ on ▪ a ▪ soc**k**.** →

**Literal Comprehension**   Reading Mastery I Seatwork

Write the sound *h* under each picture if the name begins with *h*. When you finish, color the pictures you wrote *h* under.

## h

**Sounds and Letters**   **Reading Mastery I Seatwork**

Cut out the words at the bottom of the page. Paste a word in each box so the sentences make sense.

dan ▪ āt<sub>e</sub> ▪ a ▪ [    ] .

mac<sub>k</sub> ▪ is ▪ his ▪ [    ] .

a ▪ cat ▪ sat ▪ in ▪ thē ▪ [    ] .

sam ▪ is ▪ on ▪ a ▪ [    ] .

thē ▪ mē<sub>a</sub>t ▪ is ▪ [    ] .

nām<sub>e</sub> | nut | hot | tē<sub>a</sub>m | sun

**Inferential Comprehension**   Reading Mastery I Seatwork

Put the words in order. Write them in the boxes. Then finish the pictures so they show what the words say.

f̄ēēt
mud
in

| f | e | e | t | ■ | i | n | ■ | m | u | d |

s̄ēēd
on
rug
a

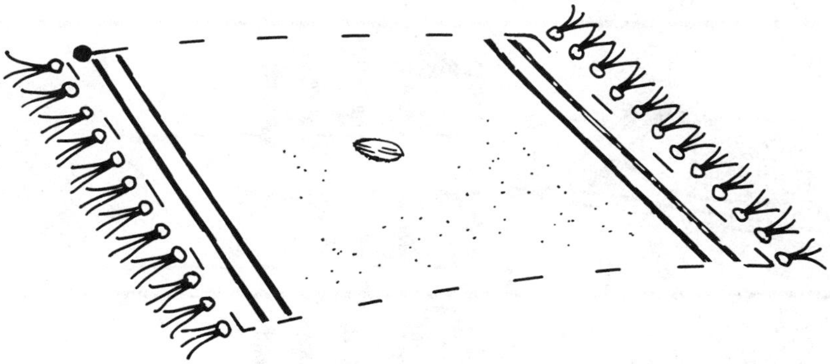

| | | | | ■ | | | ■ | | ■ | | | |

mitt
a
has
h̄ē

| | | ■ | | | | ■ | | ■ | | | |

Copy the word that goes with each picture. Then color all the pictures.

hut
hot ⟶ _____

cat
rat ⟶ _____

rug
ram ⟶ _____

fun
sun ⟶ _____

not
nut ⟶ _____

fēēt
fēēd ⟶ _____

**Words**  Reading Mastery I Seatwork

Circle the sentence that tells about each picture. When you finish, color all the pictures.

**it ▪ is ▪ hot.**

**it ▪ is ▪ not ▪ hot.**

**hē ▪ is ▪ on ▪ a ▪ roc k.**

**hē ▪ is ▪ on ▪ a ▪ fan.**

**mac k ▪ is ▪ mē a n.**

**mac k ▪ is ▪ sad.**

**dan ▪ has ▪ a ▪ fin.**

**dan ▪ has ▪ a ▪ fan.**

**Literal Comprehension**   **Reading Mastery I Seatwork**

Copy each sentence next to the picture it matches.  Then color the pictures.

# sam ▪ is ▪ a ▪ cat.
# sam ▪ is ▪ a ▪ man.
# sam ▪ is ▪ a ▪ ram.

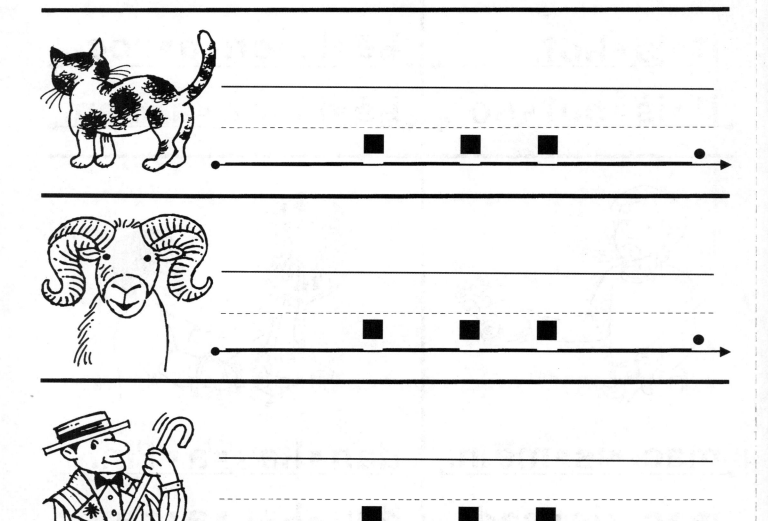

**Sentences**    Reading Mastery I Seatwork

Trace the words on the page. Then look for those things in the picture. Copy the words for the things you find.

cat

feet

sun

ram

fan

hut

mitt

mud

   **Words**   Reading Mastery I Seatwork

Copy the word that goes with each picture. Then color all the pictures.

| | | |
|---|---|---|
| | **ant** → | _____ |
| | **am** → | _____→ |
| | **dim** → | _____ |
| | **dan** → | _____→ |
| | **fat** → | _____ |
| | **fan** → | _____→ |
| | **ham** → | _____ |
| | **has** → | _____→ |
| | **miss** → | _____ |
| | **mitt** → | _____→ |
| | **ran** → | _____ |
| | **ram** → | _____→ |

Cut out the words at the bottom of the page. Paste a word in each box so the sentences make sense.

sam ▪ ran ▪ in ▪ thē ▪ ☐ .

hē ▪ āt₍ₑ₎ ▪ hot ▪ ☐ .

thē ▪ ram ▪ has ▪ fat ▪ ☐ .

thē ▪ socₖ ▪ will ▪ not ▪ ☐ .

macₖ ▪ sat ▪ on ▪ a ▪ ☐ .

| mud | fit | fēēt | rocₖ | mēₐt |

**Inferential Comprehension**   Reading Mastery I Seatwork

Make the sentences match the pictures. Circle the right word to finish each sentence. When you finish, color the pictures.

**sam ▪ is ▪** ▬▬▬▬▬▬▬ .

sad　　mad　　fat

**mac_k ▪ has ▪ a ▪** ▬▬▬▬▬ .

cat　　hat　　fat

**dan ▪ is ▪ a ▪ mē_an ▪** ▬▬▬▬ .

man　　fan　　tan

**a ▪ ram ▪ is ▪ in ▪** ▬▬▬▬▬ .

sun　　mud　　hut

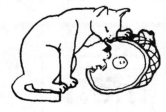

**a ▪ cat ▪ āt_e ▪ a ▪** ▬▬▬▬▬ .

sam　　ham　　ram

　　**Literal Comprehension**　　Reading Mastery I Seatwork

Cut out the words at the bottom of the page. Paste them on the train parts so the words make sentences.
When you finish, turn your paper over and draw a picture of one of your sentences.

■hit■

■māde■

■had■

an■ant

a■mud■hut.

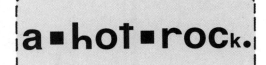
a■hot■rock.

a■mēan■tēam

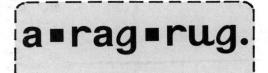
a■rag■rug.

a■mad■ram

Read the word on the arrow at the beginning of each row of letters. That word is hidden in the row of letters. Find the hidden words and circle them. The first row is already done. After you find the hidden words, draw a picture of the last two words—*his hand.*

| rut → | r | r | u | t | l | g | u | t | r |
| fig → | ā | o | f | n | g | f | i | g | i |
| nut → | i | f | n | u | t | t | u | n | m |
| sag → | s | a | g | s | m | a | g | t | g |
| run → | ē | n | r | i | r | u | n | l | r |
| ant → | t | n | a | n | m | a | a | n | t |
| his → | f | h | h | i | s | u | s | d | i |
| hand → | d | h | u | h | a | n | d | o | h |

his·hand →

Put the words in order. Write them in the boxes. Then finish the pictures so they show what the words say.

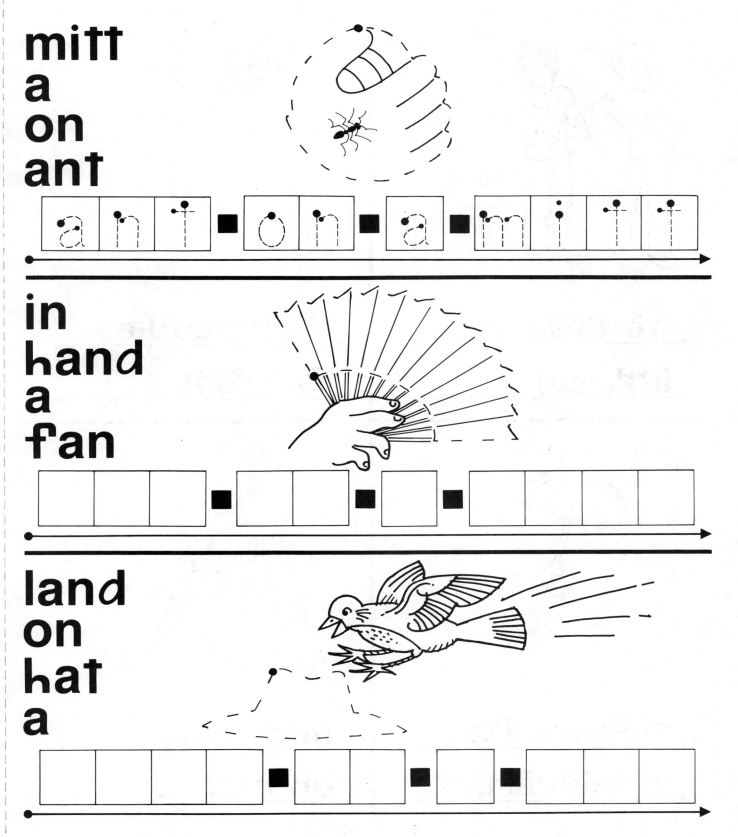

**mitt**
**a**
**on**
**ant**

**in**
**hand**
**a**
**fan**

**land**
**on**
**hat**
**a**

**Literal Comprehension**   Reading Mastery I Seatwork

There's a part missing from each picture on this page.  Read the sentences to find out what parts are missing.
Draw in the missing parts.  Then color all the pictures.

**wē·fēēd·thē**

**littlₑ·cat.**

**that·man·has**

**fat·fēēt.**

**shē·has·fun**

**in·thē·rāᵢn.**

**macₖ·sat**

**on·a·rocₖ.**

Literal Comprehension    Reading Mastery I Seatwork

Trace the words on the page. Then look for those things in the picture. Copy the words for the things you find.

fin

rug

man

hat

ham

hand

sand

sun

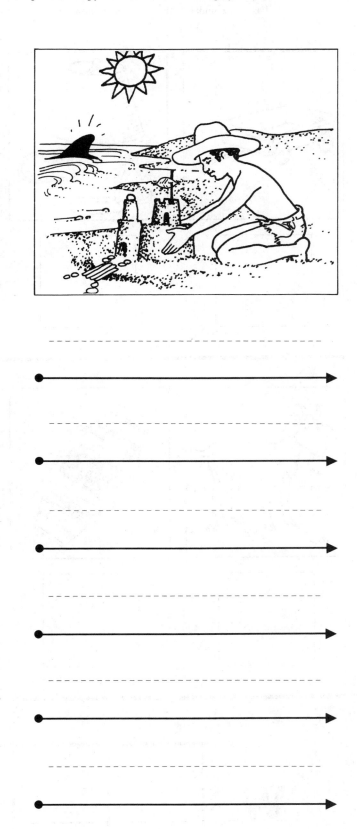

Copy the sound *www* in each box at the bottom of the page. Then cut out the boxes that have *www*.
Paste one under each picture that shows a word that begins with *www*.

**Sounds and Letters**   Reading Mastery I Seatwork

Circle the sentence that tells about each picture. When you finish, color all the pictures.

shē has māil.

shē has a locₖ.

thē rug is his.

thē socₖ is his.

it is on a hat.

it is on a hut.

ron is in thē sun.

ron is in thē mud.

**Literal Comprehension**    Reading Mastery I Seatwork

Cut out the words at the bottom of the page. Paste each word in the box next to the picture it matches. Then copy the words.

Copy each sentence next to the picture it matches.  Then color the pictures.

## shē has a cat.
## shē has a fan.
## shē has a rug.

Sentences    Reading Mastery I Seatwork

Write the sound *shshsh* under each picture if the name begins with *shshsh*. When you finish, color the pictures you wrote *shshsh* under.

**sh**

**7**

**Sounds and Letters**   Reading Mastery I Seatwork

Trace the words on the page. Then look for those things in the picture. Copy the words for the things you find.

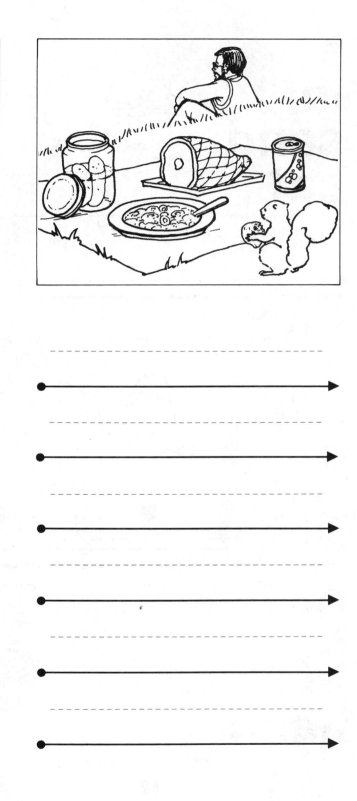

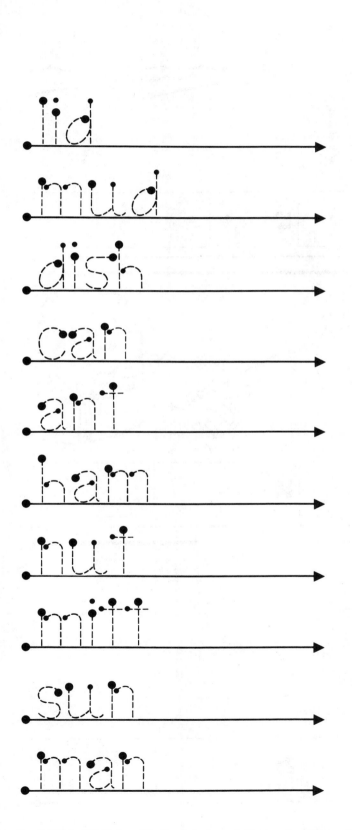

Put the words in order. Write them in the boxes. Then finish the pictures so they show what the words say.

a
in
sand
cat

| a | | c | a | t | | i | n | | s | a | n | d |

hut
a
hill
on

nut
a
in
hand

**Literal Comprehension**   Reading Mastery I Seatwork

There's a part missing from each picture on this page.  Read the sentences to find out what parts are missing.  Draw in the missing parts.  Then color all the pictures.

**that cat has** →

**littlₑ ēₐrs.**

**thē hut is on** →

**thē hill.** →

**dan got a fish.** →

**thē ant runs** →

**on a dish.** →

**Literal Comprehension**     Reading Mastery I Seatwork

Make each word match the picture next to it. Choose the correct sound from the box and write it in the blank.

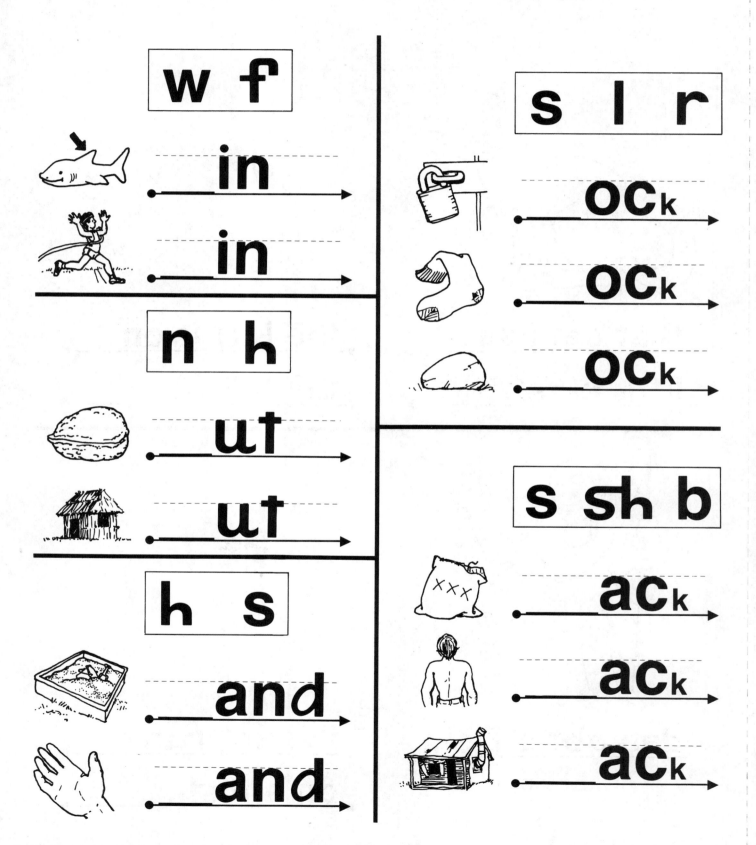

Copy each sentence next to the picture it matches.  Then color the pictures.

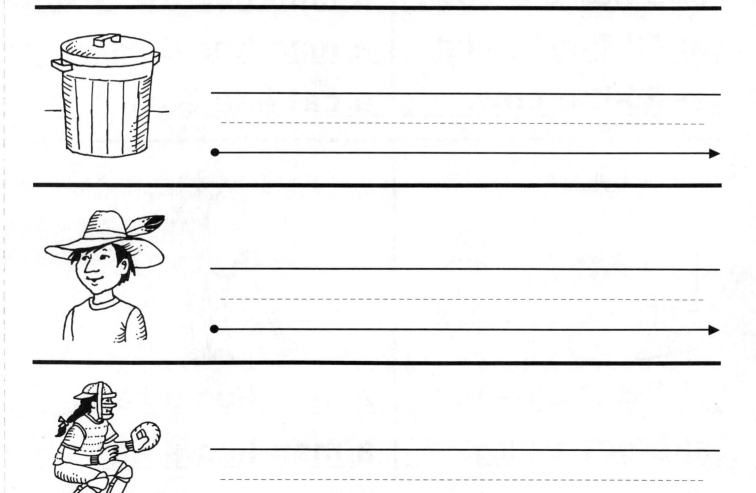

shē has a mitt.

it has a lid.

hē has a hat.

Circle the sentence that tells about each picture. When you finish, color all the pictures.

• shē hēₐrs a cow.

• shē hēₐrs a fish.

• shē hit a cow.

• a man has nō ēₐrs.

• a man has ēₐrs.

• a cat has ēₐrs.

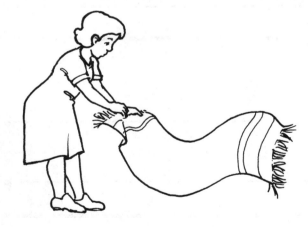

• shē got a ham.

• shē got a rug.

• shē got a nut.

• a man has a ram.

• a man has a hat.

• a man has a cat.

**Literal Comprehension**  Reading Mastery I Seatwork

Read the word on the arrow at the beginning of each row of letters. That word is hidden in the row of letters. Find the hidden words and circle them. The first row is already done. After you find the hidden words, draw a picture of the last word—*cow.*

| win → | (w  i  n) | l | o | w | i | r | w |
|---|---|---|---|---|---|---|---|
| sun → | s  g  s | u | n | s | r | u | s |
| lid → | g  l  i | d | d | l | i | u | b |
| got → | n  m  t | g | i | g | o | t | o |
| did → | i  d  c | d | i | d | a | u | i |
| mom → | k  m  o | ē | t | h | m | o | m |
| digs → | s  g  c | d | i | g | s | t | i |
| cow → | o  a  w | o | c | o | w | c | r |

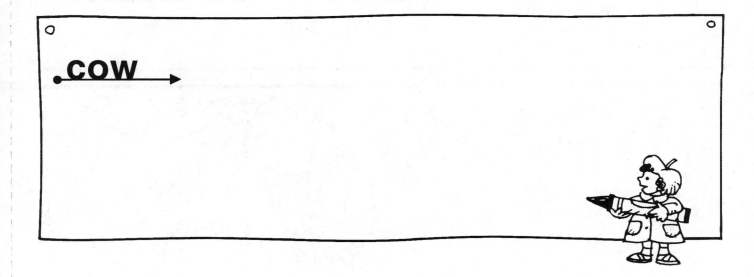

**COW →**

**Words**     Reading Mastery I Seatwork

Unscramble each set of words to make a sentence. The first word in each sentence is given to you.
When you finish, color the picture.

## sad. sam is

 _____

## has a hut. dan

 _____

## fat. thē is ram

 _____

## thē is hot. sun

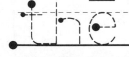 _____

**Sentences**   **Reading Mastery I Seatwork**

There's a part missing from each picture on this page. Read the sentences to find out what parts are missing. Draw in the missing parts. Then color all the pictures.

**this man has
a hat on.**

**a shac<sub>k</sub> is
nē<sub>a</sub>r thē lāk<sub>e</sub>.**

**thē cat sat
on thē gāt<sub>e</sub>.**

**thē cow lic<sub>k</sub>s
thē sad man.**

Make each word match the picture next to it. Choose the correct sound from the box and write it in the blank.

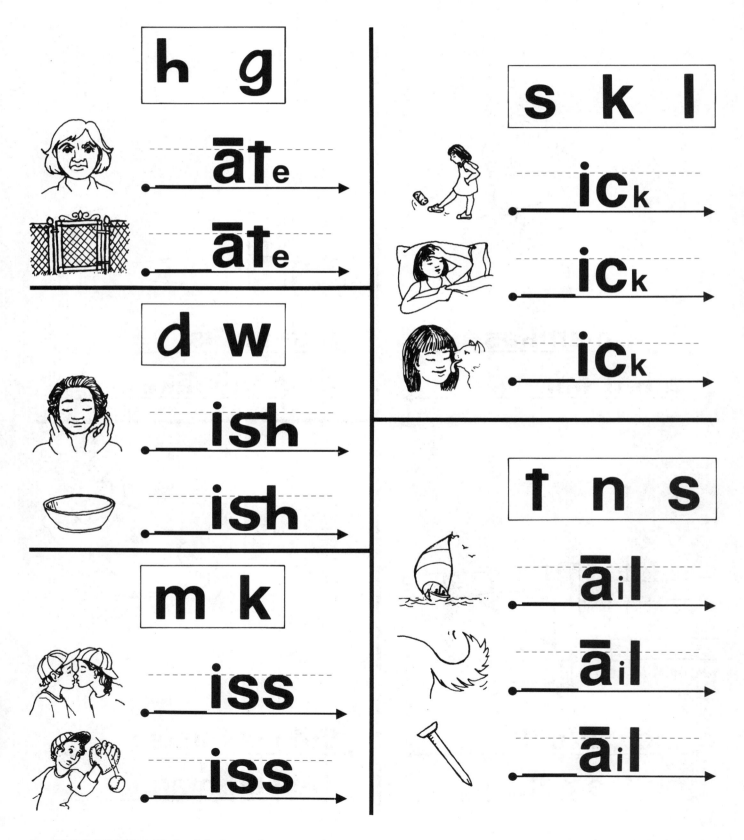

| h g |
|---|
| āt_e |
| āt_e |

| d w |
|---|
| ish |
| ish |

| m k |
|---|
| iss |
| iss |

| s k l |
|---|
| ic_k |
| ic_k |
| ic_k |

| t n s |
|---|
| āil |
| āil |
| āil |

Copy each sentence next to the picture it matches. Then color the pictures.

# a cat is fat.

# a ram is fat.

# a rat is not fat.

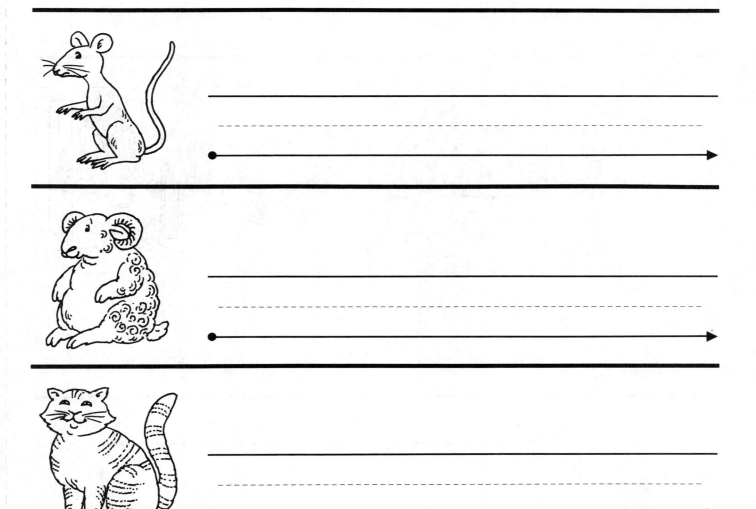

Copy the sound *k* in each box at the bottom of the page. Then cut out the boxes that have *k*. Paste one under each picture that shows a word that begins with *k*.

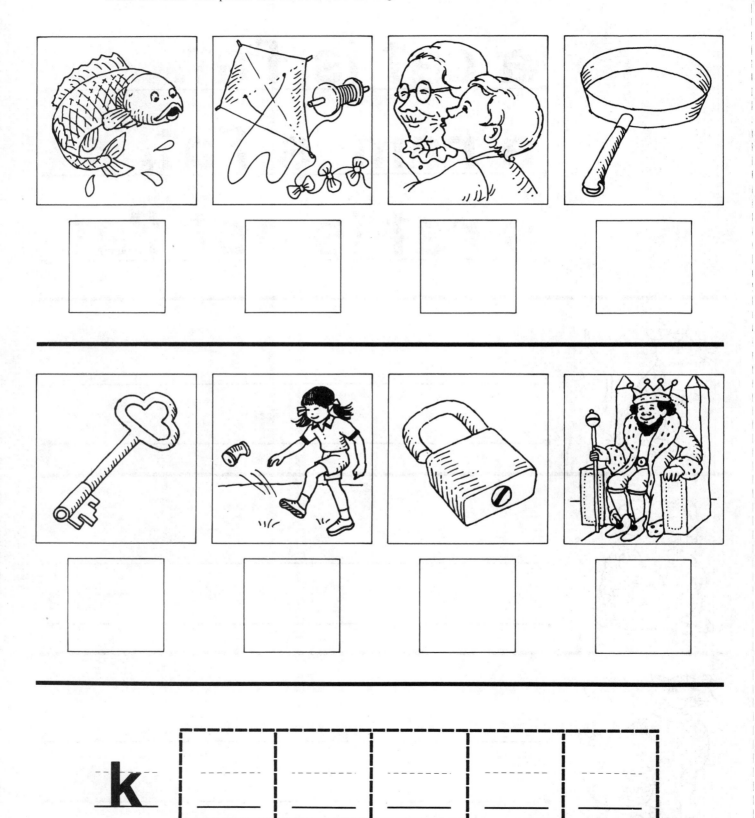

k

**Sounds and Letters** **Reading Mastery I Seatwork**

Make the sentences match the pictures. Circle the right word to finish each sentence. When you finish, color the pictures.

**1.** mom has a ▬▬▬▬▬.

fish    sacₖ    wish

**2.** hit thē ▬▬▬▬▬▬▬.

sāil    cat    nāil

**3.** it is a hot ▬▬▬▬▬▬.

rocₖ    shot    dish

**4.** wē can ▬▬▬▬▬▬▬.

rocₖ    rēad    ēat

**5.** sit on thē ▬▬▬▬▬▬.

nut    gāmₑ    gātₑ

**6.** thē hat is on a ▬▬▬▬.

hand    sēat    rat

Literal Comprehension    Reading Mastery I Seatwork

Unscramble each set of letters to make a word. Write the word on the line. The first letter of each word you will write is already shown. When you finish, draw a picture of the word at the bottom of the page. Color your picture.

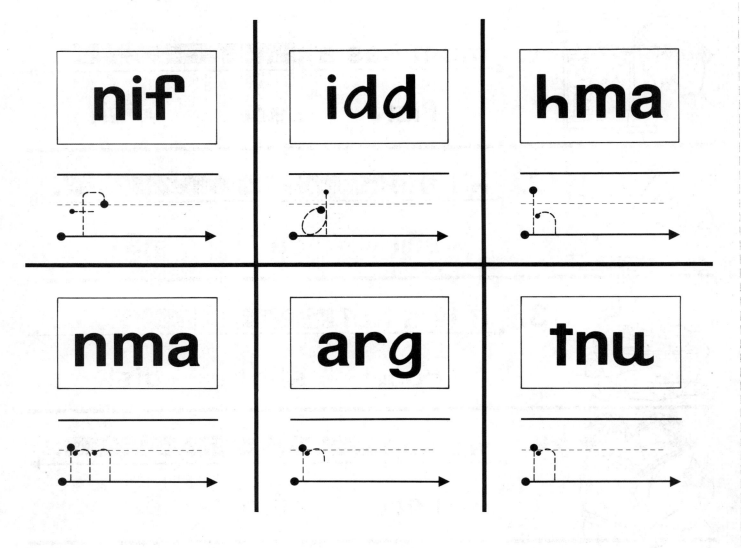

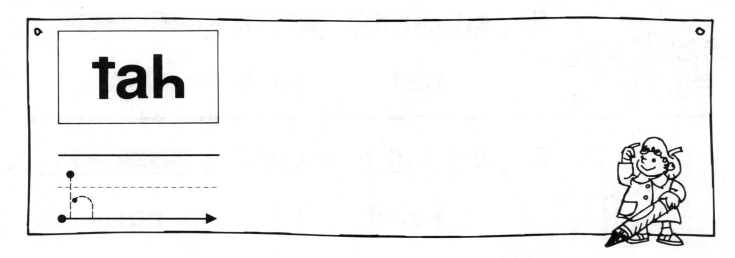

Unscramble each set of words to make a sentence. The first word in each sentence is given to you.
When you finish, color the picture.

**man the is old.**

the

**cow the fat. is**

the

**the hat sold. was**

the

**is mad. the man**

the

There's a part missing from each picture on this page. Read the sentences to find out what parts are missing. Draw in the missing parts. Then color all the pictures.

• **thē fish is**
**in thē lāke.** ➤

• **dan has an ant**
**on his nōse.** ➤

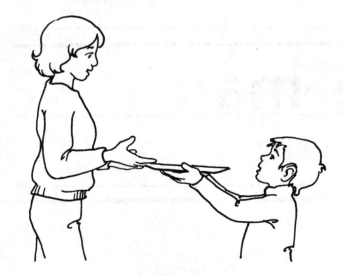

• **hē gāve his**
**mom a cāke.** ➤

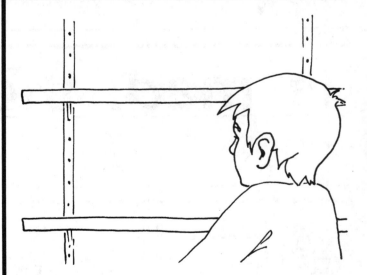

• **sam has lots**
**of hats.** ➤

**Literal Comprehension**   Reading Mastery I Seatwork

Make each word match the picture next to it. Choose the correct sound from the box and write it in the blank.

Copy the word that goes with each picture. Then color all the pictures.

**can** →
**cow** →
_____

**fan** →
**fat** →
_____

**hut** →
**hug** →
_____

**mud** →
**mom** →
_____

**hat** →
**has** →
_____

**sum** →
**sun** →
_____

Read the sentences.  Circle *yes* if a sentence is right or *no* if a sentence is not right.  When you finish all the sentences, color the picture.

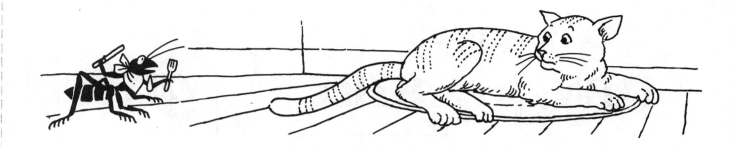

1. an ant can ēₐt a cat. •yes •nō

2. a cow has a taiil. •yes •nō

3. ham is mēₐt. •yes •nō

4. a man can run. •yes •nō

5. a fish has fēēt. •yes •nō

6. rats can rēₐd. •yes •nō

7. a dish can kiss. •yes •nō

8. a cat has ēₐrs. •yes •nō

9. a cop can hōld a mop. •yes •nō

Unscramble each set of letters to make a word. Write the word on the line. The first letter of each word you will write is already shown. When you finish, draw a picture of the word at the bottom of the page. Color your picture.

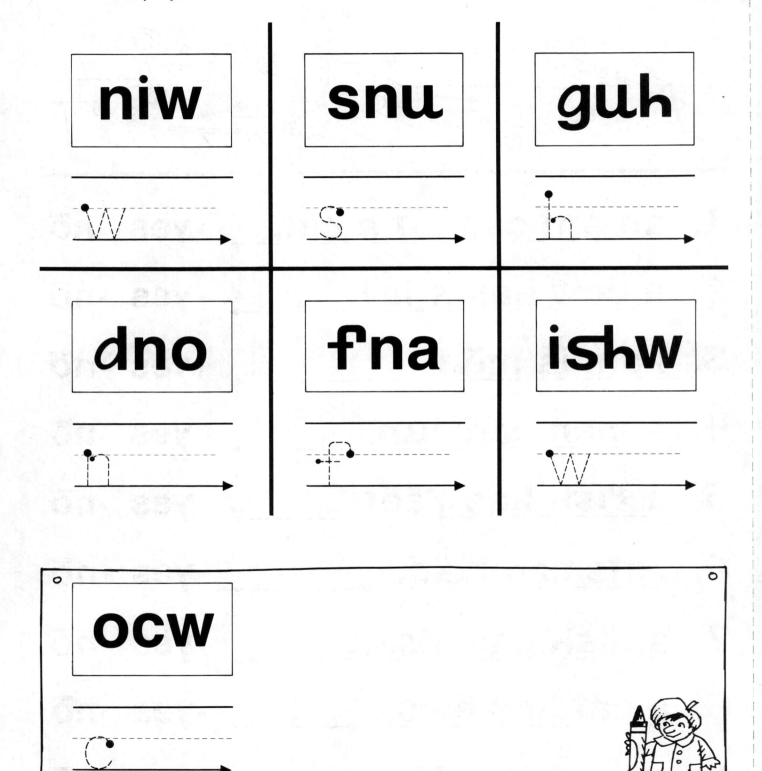

niw

w

snu

s

guh

h

dno

n

fna

f

ishw

w

ocw

c

Unscramble each set of words to make a sentence. The first word in each sentence is given to you.
When you finish, color the picture.

**cop. a mom is**

 _____→

**has dog. a shē**

 _____→

**sand. in sits dan**

dan _____→

**for hē fun. digs**

hē _____→

**Sentences**   Reading Mastery I Seatwork

Cut out the words at the bottom of the page. Paste a word in each box so the sentences make sense.

I have to feed the [ ].

the ship has a [ ].

the kitten sat on his [ ].

he hears with his [ ].

she made a [ ].

| tāil | sāil | cāke | cats | ēars |

**Inferential Comprehension**   Reading Mastery I Seatwork

Make each word match the picture next to it. Choose the correct sound from the box and write it in the blank.

| r  h | | l  d |
|---|---|---|
| ____ **ug** → | | ____ **og** → |
| ____ **ug** → | | ____ **og** → |

| h  p | | g  c |
|---|---|---|
| ____ **ot** → | | ____ **ōat** → |
| ____ **ot** → | | ____ **ōat** → |

| s  f | | m  s |
|---|---|---|
| ____ **ēēd** → | | ____ **ēat** → |
| ____ **ēēd** → | | ____ **ēat** → |

**Words**  Reading Mastery I Seatwork

Circle the sentence that tells about each picture. When you finish, color all the pictures.

shē āte a fish. →

shē āte mēat. →

shē āte a dish. →

this dog is fat. →

this dog is mēan. →

this dog is sad. →

kick thē top. →

kick thē car. →

kick thē can. →

wē have a cōat. →

wē have a gōat. →

wē have a gāte. →

**Literal Comprehension**   **Reading Mastery I Seatwork**

Unscramble each set of letters to make a word. Write the word on the line. The first letter of each word you will write is already shown. When you finish, draw a picture of the word at the bottom of the page. Color your picture.

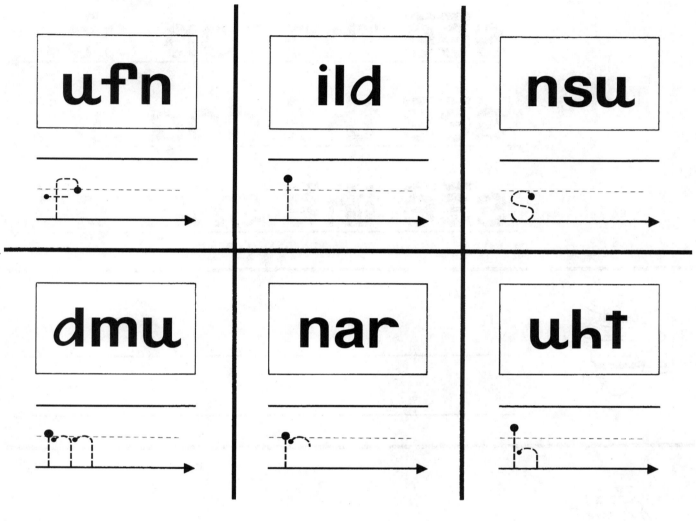

**Words     Reading Mastery I Seatwork**

Copy each sentence next to the picture it matches. Then color the pictures.

sēē thē top gō.

sēē thē dog gō.

sēē thē ship gō.

     **Sentences**    Reading Mastery I Seatwork

There's a part missing from each picture on this page. Read the sentences to find out what parts are missing. Draw in the missing parts. Then color all the pictures.

## a kitten is on
## top of the car.

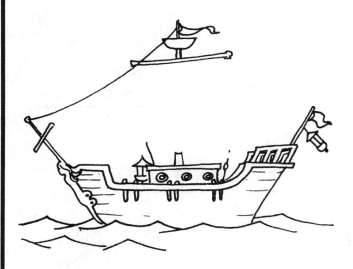

## thē ship has a
## sāil.

## thē cop has a
## socκ in his hand.

## thē girl has
## an ōld gōaṭ.

**Literal Comprehension**   Reading Mastery I Seatwork

Write the sound *p* under each picture if the name begins with *p*. When you finish, color the pictures you wrote *p* under.

**p**

Make each word match the picture next to it. Choose the correct sound from the box and write it in the blank.

| f  d |

____ ish

____ ish

| sh  w |

____ āve

____ āve

| r  h |

____ ug

____ ug

| l  k  s |

____ ick

____ ick

____ ick

| c  m  t |

____ op

____ op

____ op

**Words**   Reading Mastery I Seatwork

Read the sentences. Circle *yes* if a sentence is right or *no* if a sentence is not right. When you finish all the sentences, color the picture.

1. a gōat can bē ōld. → •yes •nō

2. a man can ēat a nut. → •yes •nō

3. rocks havₑ ēars. → •yes •nō

4. socks havₑ tēēth. → •yes •nō

5. rāin will gō down. → •yes •nō

6. a man can shāvₑ. → •yes •nō

7. a mop can hug. → •yes •nō

8. a gātₑ can havₑ a lock. → •yes •nō

9. a kitten has a nōsₑ. → •yes •nō

Sentences  Reading Mastery I Seatwork

Cut out the words at the bottom of the page. Paste a word in each box so the sentences make sense.

the cows āt<sub>e</sub> ☐.

his tē<sub>a</sub>m will win the ☐.

pigs can not ☐.

the kitten is ☐.

the girl can sēē ☐.

ō<sub>a</sub>ts | far | gām<sub>e</sub> | littl<sub>e</sub> | rē<sub>a</sub>d

**Inferential Comprehension**    Reading Mastery I Seatwork

Finish each sentence with a word from the bottom of the page. Then write those words in the crossword puzzle.
The number for each word shows where it goes in the crossword puzzle. The arrow for each number shows
if the word goes across or down. The word for sentence one is already written in the crossword puzzle.

1. **fēēd the** _____.

2. **gō up to the** _____.

3. **dan** _____.

4. **mom will ēₐt** _____.

5. **soсₖs fit on** _____.

4 **nuts**

1 **cows**

2 **top**

3 **runs**

5 **fēēt**

Write the sound *ch* under each picture if the name begins with *ch*. When you finish, color the pictures you wrote *ch* under.

# ch

**Sounds and Letters     Reading Mastery I Seatwork**

Unscramble each set of words to make a sentence. The first word in each sentence is given to you.
When you finish, color the picture.

**sal mop. has a** →

 sal →

**shē with sam. is** →

 shē →

**hug I cat. the** →

I →

**mitt. the dan wins** →

 dan →

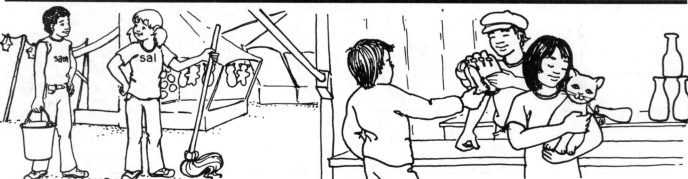

Sentences   Reading Mastery I Seatwork

Cut out the words at the bottom of the page. Paste a word in each box so the sentences make sense.

hē āte the [ ].

the dog had a little [ ].

a car cāme down the [ ].

the duck will get [ ].

shē will fish in the [ ].

| rōad | wet | nōse | lāke | chips |

**Inferential Comprehension**    **Reading Mastery I Seatwork**

Name _____ 

Trace the words on the page. Then look for those things in the picture. Copy the words for the things you find.

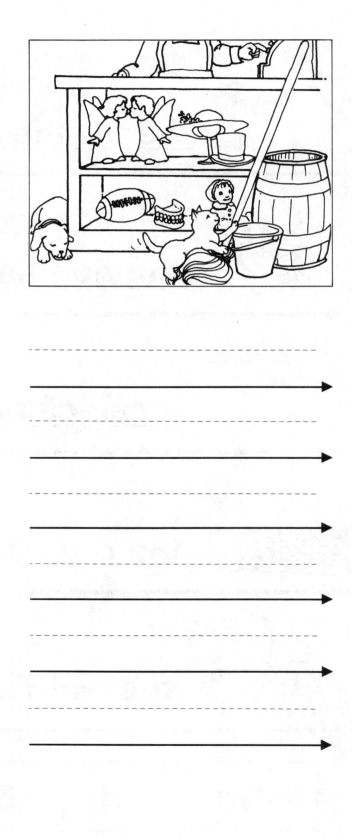

hats ⟶

hug ⟶

kitten ⟶

fog ⟶

mop ⟶

dog ⟶

top ⟶

teeth ⟶

kiss ⟶

log ⟶

Read the sentences. Circle *yes* if a sentence is right or *no* if a sentence is not right. When you finish all the sentences, color the picture.

1. <u>cars can gō on rōads.</u>  •yes •nō

2. <u>lākes are wet.</u>  •yes •nō

3. <u>a rug has a hand.</u>  •yes •nō

4. <u>a dish has a tāil.</u>  •yes •nō

5. <u>a kitten is a little cat.</u>  •yes •nō

6. <u>a pig has a fin.</u>  •yes •nō

7. <u>a nāil has ēars.</u>  •yes •nō

8. <u>bugs can sit on logs.</u>  •yes •nō

9. <u>fish can park cars.</u>  •yes •nō

Sentences   Reading Mastery I Seatwork

Read the story.  Then write the correct word to finish each sentence.  When you finish, draw a picture of the *hut* from the story.

# I have a little hut. it is on a hill. the little hut is old. I will paint it red.

1. I have a little _____.
2. the hut is on a _____.
3. the little hut is _____.
4. I will paint it _____.

the hut on a hill →

**Literal Comprehension**    Reading Mastery I Seatwork

Choose the right arrow for each picture. Copy the words on the bottom arrow.
When you finish, color the pictures.

## bed in pet →

## pet in bed →

_ _ _ _ _ _ _ _ _ _ _ _ _ _ _ _ _ _

_____ →

## ten on can →

## can on ten →

_ _ _ _ _ _ _ _ _ _ _ _ _ _ _ _ _ _

_____ →

## ship on men →

## men on ship →

_ _ _ _ _ _ _ _ _ _ _ _ _ _ _ _ _ _

_____ →

Copy each sentence next to the picture it matches.  Then color the pictures.

# the sun is hot.

# the log is hot.

# the pot is hot.

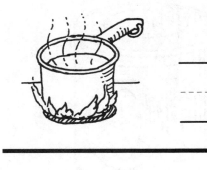

**Sentences** **Reading Mastery I Seatwork**

Write the sound *b* under each picture if the name begins with *b*. When you finish, color the pictures you wrote *b* under.

**b**

**Sounds and Letters**   **Reading Mastery I Seatwork**

Finish each sentence with a word from the bottom of the page. Then write those words in the crossword puzzle.
The number for each word shows where it goes in the crossword puzzle. The arrow for each number shows
if the word goes across or down. The word for sentence one is already written in the crossword puzzle.

# l. mom likes _____.

# 2. the dog _____.

# 3. ann is a _____.

# 4. the pot has a _____.

# 5. I run up the _____.

3 **girl**

2 **digs**

4 **lid**

5 **hill**

l **hats**

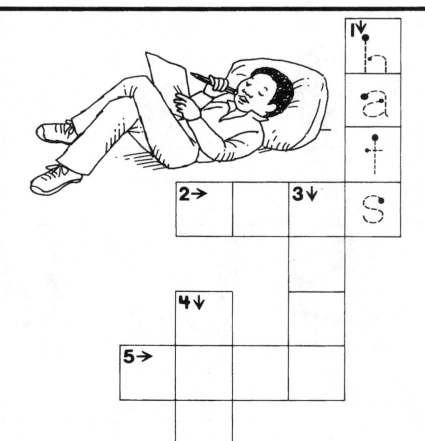

Words  Reading Mastery I Seatwork

Read the sentences.  Circle *yes* if a sentence is right or *no* if a sentence is not right.  When you finish all the sentences, color the picture.

1. wē can sit on a rug. → •yes •nō

2. the sun is hot. → •yes •nō

3. bugs līke to shop. → •yes •nō

4. rāin can bē cōld. → •yes •nō

5. a pot can have a lid. → •yes •nō

6. a lock can hēar. → •yes •nō

7. cows can kick. → •yes •nō

8. a pig has a nōse. → •yes •nō

9. rocks nēēd slēēp. → •yes •nō

Sentences    Reading Mastery I Seatwork

Copy the word that goes with each picture.  Then color all the pictures.

| | | |
|---|---|---|
| | **sit** → | _____ |
| | **slid** → | - - - - - - - - - → |
| | **bug** → | _____ |
| | **bōy** → | - - - - - - - - - → |
| | **stop** → | _____ |
| | **ship** → | - - - - - - - - - → |
| | **dig** → | _____ |
| | **dim** → | - - - - - - - - - → |
| | **slēēp** → | _____ |
| | **talk** → | - - - - - - - - - → |
| | **corn** → | _____ |
| | **cow** → | - - - - - - - - - → |

**Words**    Reading Mastery I Seatwork

Read the story. Then write the correct word to finish each sentence. When you finish, draw a picture of *Sam* and *Dan* from the story.

sam is a man. his cat is dan. sam sleeps in a bed. his cat sleeps on a rug.

1. sam is a _____.

2. dan is a _____.

3. sam sleeps in a _____.

4. dan sleeps on a _____.

sam and dan

**Literal Comprehension**   **Reading Mastery I Seatwork**

Cut out the words at the bottom of the page.  Paste each word in the box next to the picture it matches.
Then copy the words.

Copy the word that goes with each picture.  Then color all the pictures.

wāvīng
dīvīng

cut
bug

hill
him

can
car

pond
pot

top
cop

Words    Reading Mastery I Seatwork

Choose the right arrow for each picture. Copy the words on the bottom arrow. When you finish, color the pictures.

## corn in cops →
## cops in corn →
-------------------------------------→

## sam hugs ram. →
## ram hugs sam. →
-------------------------------------→

## dish on fish →
## fish on dish →
-------------------------------------→

**Literal Comprehension** Reading Mastery I Seatwork

Read the story and the sentences below it. Circle *yes* or *no* for each sentence.
When you finish, color the picture.

ann and al are little bugs. they live in a hole in a log. they read and eat in the hole. they sleep on old socks.

1. ann is a little bug. →  •yes  •no

2. al is a big bug. →  •yes  •no

3. they live in a hole. →  •yes  •no

4. the hole is in a hut. →  •yes  •no

5. ann and al read and eat. →  •yes  •no

6. they sleep on old rocks. →  •yes  •no

**Literal Comprehension**  Reading Mastery I Seatwork

Finish each sentence with a word from the bottom of the page. Then write those words in the crossword puzzle.
The number for each word shows where it goes in the crossword puzzle. The arrow for each number shows
if the word goes across or down. The word for sentence one is already written in the crossword puzzle.

1. they sleep in _____.

2. the car is _____.

3. do not hit his _____.

4. cows live on _____.

5. fish live in _____.

3 hand
5 ponds
1 beds
4 farms
2 red

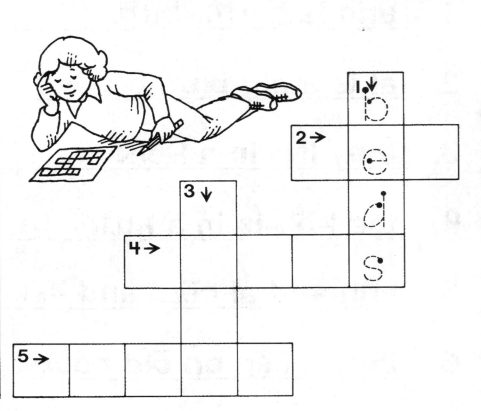

Trace the words on the page. Then look for those things in the picture. Copy the words for the things you find.

tub ————————————————➤

pig ————————————————➤

cow ————————————————➤

rabbit ————————————————➤

bug ————————————————➤

boy ————————————————➤

pot ————————————————➤

pond ————————————————➤

girl ————————————————➤

sheep ————————————————➤

Read the story. Then write the correct word to finish each sentence. When you finish, draw a picture of *Mack* and *Sal* from the story.

mack and sal are pigs.

they live on a farm.

they sit in the mud.

they ēat lots of corn.

1. mack and sal are _____.

2. they live on a _____.

3. they sit in the _____.

4. they eat lots of _____.

mack and sal →

Literal Comprehension    Reading Mastery 1 Seatwork

Cut out the faces at the bottom of the page. Paste each face on the head next to the right story.

shē kicks the gāte. ⟶

shē hits her pet pig. ⟶

the girl is mēan. ⟶

the bōy is sad. ⟶

hē can not fīnd his dog. ⟶

sēē the tēar. ⟶

mȳ brother līkes cats. ⟶

hē got a littl e kitten. ⟶

wow. ⟶

I āte lots of nuts. ⟶

now I fēēl sick. ⟶

I nēēd to slēēp. ⟶

**Inferential Comprehension** Reading Mastery I Seatwork

Finish each sentence with a word from the bottom of the page. Then write those words in the crossword puzzle.
The number for each word shows where it goes in the crossword puzzle. The arrow for each number shows
if the word goes across or down. The word for sentence one is already written in the crossword puzzle.

1. pigs ēat _____ .

2. hop līke a _____ .

3. pāint the _____ .

4. wē walk on _____ .

5. his tēam _____ .

1 corn
3 barn
4 rugs
2 frog
5 wins

Words   Reading Mastery I Seatwork

Read the story and the sentences below it. Circle *yes* or *no* for each sentence.
When you finish, color the picture.

a bug lived on a lēaf. a rabbit cāme to ēat the lēaf. "nō," said the bug, "I love this lēaf." sō the bug āte the lēaf.

1. a rabbit lived on a bug.        •yes  •nō

2. a bug lived on a lēaf.         •yes  •nō

3. the rabbit cāme to ēat.        •yes  •nō

4. the bug āte the rabbit.        •yes  •nō

5. the rabbit āte the lēaf.        •yes  •nō

Unscramble each set of words to make a sentence. The first word in each sentence is given to you.
When you finish, color the picture

**a** girl digging. is

a ➝

**the** cold. is boy

the ➝

**brother.** her hē is

he ➝

**sēē** a they rabbit.

they ➝

Cut out the words at the bottom of the page. Paste each word in the box next to the picture it matches.
Then copy the words.

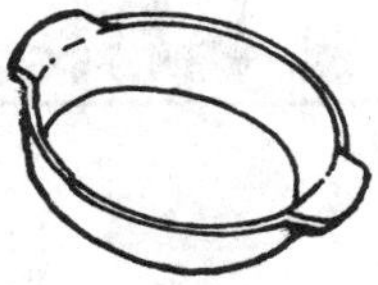

| | |
|---|---|
| | |

dish

brush

deer

ship

pig

girl

Cut out the pictures at the bottom of the page.  Paste each picture in the box next to the sentence it goes with.

1.  let's pāint the room red. ⟶

2.  I must dig a hōle. ⟶

3.  I līke to rēad. ⟶

4.  I have a sōre leg. ⟶

5.  I love to gō shopping. ⟶

**Inferential Comprehension**    Reading Mastery I Seatwork

Read the sentences. Circle *yes* if a sentence is right or *no* if a sentence is not right. When you finish all the sentences, color the picture.

1. a frog līkes to jump.  •yes •nō

2. gōats slēēp in a pond.  •yes •nō

3. gum can swim.  •yes •nō

4. cows live on farms.  •yes •nō

5. a broom has ten ēars.  •yes •nō

6. a lēaf can run.  •yes •nō

7. a fox līkes shopping.  •yes •nō

8. an ēagle can ēat.  •yes •nō

9. it is dark in a cāve.  •yes •nō

Read the story.  Then write the correct word to finish each sentence.  When you finish, draw a picture of *Ann* and *Dan* from the story.

ann is a girl. her brother is dan. they līke to rīde the bus. they gō to the park.

1. ann is a _____.

2. dan is her _____.

3. they rīde the _____.

4. they gō to the _____.

ann and dan

**Literal Comprehension**  **Reading Mastery I Seatwork**

Unscramble each set of letters to make a word. Write the word on the line. The first letter of each word you will write is already shown. When you finish, draw a picture of the word at the bottom of the page. Color your picture.

**dre**

r→

**gol**

l→

**bxo**

b→

**gip**

p→

**ocp**

c→

**lōd**

ō→

**ugb**

b→

**Words**   Reading Mastery I Seatwork

Cut out the faces at the bottom of the page. Paste each face on the head next to the right story.

hē māde some cākes. →

a gōat āte the cākes. →

hē is mad. →

---

shē went shopping. →

shē walked a lot. →

now shē must slēēp. →

---

I fell down. →

I have a sōre arm. →

I am sad. →

---

I am rīding a bīke. →

I līke to rīde a bīke. →

I am having fun. →

**Inferential Comprehension**   Reading Mastery I Seatwork

Copy the word that goes with each picture. Then color all the pictures.

**box** →

**boy** →

_____

**bad** →

**broom** →

_____

**mop** →

**moon** →

_____

**pool** →

**pot** →

_____

**fox** →

**for** →

_____

**run** →

**room** →

Words   Reading Mastery I Seatwork

Finish each sentence with a word from the bottom of the page. Then write those words in the crossword puzzle.
The number for each word shows where it goes in the crossword puzzle. The arrow for each number shows
if the word goes across or down. The word for sentence one is already written in the crossword puzzle.

1. they rīde in _____ .

2. the room is _____ .

3. fish ēat _____ .

4. the rabbit _____ .

5. dogs are fīne _____ .

3 **bugs**

1 **cars**

2 **dark**

5 **pets**

4 **jumps**

Read the story. Then write the correct word to finish each sentence. When you finish, draw a picture of the *digging dogs* from the story.

**the dogs are digging.**
**they dig a hole in the**
**yard. dogs like to dig.**
**they dig for fun.**

1. **the dogs are** _____ .
2. **a hole is in the** _____ .
3. **dogs like to** _____ .
4. **they dig for** _____ .

the digging dogs →

**Literal Comprehension**   Reading Mastery I Seatwork

Cut out the pictures at the bottom of the page.  Paste each picture in the box next to the sentence it goes with.

1.  I will eat fish. ⟶

2.  wher$_e$ is the swimming pool? ⟶

3.  I went to the moon. ⟶

4.  m̄y cat līk$_e$s mē a lot. ⟶

5.  m̄y hōm$_e$ is on a farm. ⟶

**Inferential Comprehension**     Reading Mastery I Seatwork

Name _____

Write the sound *g* under each picture if the name begins with *g*. When you finish, color the pictures you wrote *g* under.

**g**

**Sounds and Letters**   Reading Mastery I Seatwork

Read the story and the sentences below it. Circle *yes* or *no* for each sentence. When you finish, color the picture.

mack was a big cat.

hē sat on an ōld hat.

the hat was on mȳ

brother pat.

a cat on a hat on pat.

1.  mack was a littlₑ cat. → •yes •nō

2.  mack sat on a hat. → •yes •nō

3.  the hat was ōld. → •yes •nō

4.  the hat was on mack. → •yes •nō

5.  pat is mȳ brother. → •yes •nō

**Literal Comprehension**   Reading Mastery I Seatwork

Copy the word that goes with each picture.  Then color all the pictures.

wē &rarr;
well &rarr;

swim &rarr;
slid &rarr;

lot &rarr;
log &rarr;

wet &rarr;
went &rarr;

hot &rarr;
how &rarr;

walk &rarr;
wish &rarr;

Words    Reading Mastery I Seatwork

Cut out the faces at the bottom of the page. Paste each face on the head next to the right story.

I had a red toy. →

mȳ dog brōke it. →

now I am mad. →

it was a hot day. →

shē was walking fast. →

shē was hot and wet. →

there is a tīger. →

will it bīte mē? →

I will run awāy. →

ann is gōing to the park. →

shē will have fun. →

look at ann smīle. →

**Inferential Comprehension**   Reading Mastery I Seatwork

# Answer Key

**Lesson 1**
*11 red stars:* 3 in sky, 1 on cactus, 1 on horse blanket, 1 for sheriff's badge, 3 on blanket, 2 on boots

**Lesson 2**
*Missing parts:* door, tree trunk, dog's body

**Lesson 3**
Pairs of trees should match.

**Lesson 4**
*11 red triangles:* 2 for owl's ears, 4 on fence posts, 1 for roof of house, 1 for witch's hat, 2 for pumpkin's eyes, 1 for pumpkin's nose

**Lesson 5**
*Missing parts:* flower top, man's shoe, bench leg

**Lesson 6**
Pairs of kites should match.

**Lesson 7**
Pairs of objects should match.

**Lesson 8**
*12 red circles:* 1 for sun, 1 for saucer sled, 3 for snowballs, 2 on girls' caps, 3 for snowman's body, 2 for snowman's buttons.

**Lesson 9**
Pairs of objects should match.

**Lesson 10**
*Missing parts:* candle, teacup, picture frame

**Lesson 11**
Pairs of objects should match.

**Lesson 12**
All *m*'s and outline of tree should be traced.

**Lesson 13**
Path connecting *a*'s and *a*'s traced.

**Lesson 14**
Letters should be traced. *m*'s should be pasted near boy's mouth; *a*'s on apples.

**Lesson 15**
*Pictures to be circled:* sock, paintbrush, coin, bird

**Lesson 16**
Letters should be traced. *m*'s should be pasted on monkey; *a*'s by arrow.

**Lesson 17**
All *s*'s and outline of sailboat should be traced.

**Lesson 18**
Picture of a brown seal

**Lesson 19**
*Pictures to be circled:* pants, paper, hair, ring

**Lesson 20**
Path connecting $\bar{e}$'s and $\bar{e}$'s traced.

**Lesson 21**
Picture of a black $\bar{e}$

**Lesson 22**
*Pictures to be circled:* necktie, plant, baseball, eating utensils

**Lesson 23**
*Pictures to be circled:* girl skating, dog chasing cat, man baking bread

**Lesson 24**
Path connecting *r*'s and *r*'s traced.

**Lesson 25**
Picture of a fish

**Lesson 26**
*Pictures to be circled:* woman shivering, dirty hands, boy falling

**Lesson 27**
*Pictures to be circled:* puddle, dress, skillet, doghouse

**Lesson 28**
*16 d's:* 4 in tree, 1 on bird, 1 on tree trunk, 4 on fence, 1 by birdbath, 1 in garden, 1 in man's hand, 1 behind cat, 2 on watering can

**Lesson 29**
Picture of a snake

**Lesson 30**
*Pictures to be circled:* lamp falling, hammer hitting finger, woman walking in the wind, girl diving

**Lesson 31**
Picture of a green dragon

**Lesson 32**
Path connecting *f*'s and *f*'s traced.

**Lesson 33**
Picture of a bird

**Lesson 34**
*Pictures to be circled:* woman knocking over cup, baby crying, tire approaching tack, hot desert scene

**Lesson 35**
Picture of an orange insect

**Lesson 36**
*1st row:* 1, 2
*2nd row:* 2, 1
*3rd row:* 2, 1
*4th row:* 1, 2

**Lesson 37**
Picture of a bear

**Lesson 38**
*1st row*: 2, 1
*2nd row*: 1, 2
*3rd row*: 2, 1
*4th row*: 1, 2

**Lesson 39**
*11 red th's*: 2 in picture, 1 on mantle,
1 on window, 1 on fireplace bricks,
1 in fire, 1 on top of television,
1 on television screen, 1 on chair,
1 on ottoman, 1 on rug

**Lesson 40**
Words should be copied.

**Lesson 41**
*1st row*: 2, 1
*2nd row*: 2, 1
*3rd row*: 1, 2
*4th row*: 1, 2

**Lesson 42**
*1st row*: 2, 1, 3
*2nd row*: 3, 2, 1
*3rd row*: 1, 3, 2
*4th row*: 2, 1, 3

**Lesson 43**
*1st row*: 2, 3, 1
*2nd row*: 1, 3, 2
*3rd row*: 3, 2, 1
*4th row*: 2, 1, 3

**Lesson 44**
Matching words should be circled.

**Lesson 45**
*1st row*: 3, 2, 1
*2nd row*: 2, 1, 3
*3rd row*: 1, 3, 2
*4th row*: 2, 1, 3

**Lesson 46**
*Sequence of pictures*: girl climbing
slide/girl in middle of slide/girl at
bottom of slide—monkey picking
banana/monkey peeling banana/
monkey eating banana

**Lesson 47**
Words should be copied.

**Lesson 48**
Picture of a kangaroo

**Lesson 49**
*Sequence of pictures*: whole
egg/beak poking out of egg/
chick outside of egg—
man entering store/ man
shopping/man leaving store

**Lesson 50**
A variety of sentences

**Lesson 51**
*t pictures*: toe, ten, tent, tail, tie

**Lesson 52**
*Sequence of pictures*: girl writing
letter/girl putting stamp on
letter/girl mailing letter—girl
boarding bus/girl riding bus/girl
getting off bus

**Lesson 53**
*Phrases to be written*: cat in can,
ram on man, seed in sam

**Lesson 54**
*n pictures*: nest, nose, needle, nine,
nail

**Lesson 55**
Matching words should be circled.

**Lesson 56**
A variety of sentences

**Lesson 57**
*Sequence of sentences*: dan is tan;
dan is mad; dan is sad.

**Lesson 58**
*c pictures*: cat, cup, camel, cake,
carrot

**Lesson 59**
Sentences should be copied.

**Lesson 60**
Matching words should be circled.

**Lesson 61**

| | |
|---|---|
| mad | rat |
| sad | cat |
| ran | meat |
| fan | seat |
| tack | sock |
| sack | rock |

**Lesson 62**
*Phrases to be written*: feet on dan,
cat on rat, fan on fin

**Lesson 63**
Sentences should be copied.

**Lesson 64**
A variety of sentences

**Lesson 65**
*Phrases to be written*: on a cat, in a
can, on a man

**Lesson 66**

| | |
|---|---|
| fan | man |
| ram | ham |
| cat | can |

**Lesson 67**
*Sequence of sentences*: the cat ran;
the cat sat; the cat fit.

**Lesson 68**

| | |
|---|---|
| ram | sun |
| ham | run |
| hit | man |
| sit | can |
| seed | tear |
| feed | fear |

**Lesson 69**
*Phrases to be written*: a seed on
sam, feed a cat, feet on a can

**Lesson 70**
*Sentences to be circled*: sam is sick;
dan had a sack; he can rock; it is on
a sock.

**Lesson 71**
*h pictures*: hat, horse, hand, house,
hanger, ham, hose, hammer, heart

**Lesson 72**

*Sequence of words to be pasted on*: nut, name, sun, team, hot

**Lesson 73**

*Phrases to be written*: feet in mud, seed on a rug, he has a mitt

**Lesson 74**

*Words to be written*: hut, rat, rug, sun, nut, feet

**Lesson 75**

*Sentences to be circled*: it is hot; he is on a rock; mack is sad; dan has a fan.

**Lesson 76**

*Sequence of sentences*: sam is a cat; sam is a ram; sam is a man.

**Lesson 77**

*Words to be written*: cat, feet, sun, fan, hut, mud

**Lesson 78**

*Words to be written*: ant, dan, fan, ham, mitt, ram

**Lesson 79**

*Sequence of words to be pasted on*: mud, meat, feet, fit, rock

**Lesson 80**

*Words to be circled*: sad, hat, man, mud, ham

**Lesson 81**

A variety of sentences

**Lesson 82**

Matching words should be circled.

**Lesson 83**

*Phrases to be written*: ant on a mitt, fan in a hand, land on a hat

**Lesson 84**

*Missing parts*: cat's body, man's feet, girl holding umbrella, rock that boy is sitting on

**Lesson 85**

*Words to be written*: fin, man, hat, hand, sand, sun

**Lesson 86**

*w pictures*: wagon, well, windmill, watch, window

**Lesson 87**

*Sentences to be circled*: she has mail; the sock is his; it is on a hat; ron is in the mud.

**Lesson 88**

| | |
|---|---|
| mitt | hut |
| sun | hand |
| man | nut |

**Lesson 89**

*Sequence of sentences*: she has a fan; she has a cat; she has a rug.

**Lesson 90**

*sh pictures*: shower, shoe, sheep, shirt, shovel, shoulder, shave, ship

**Lesson 91**

*Words to be written:* lid, dish, can, ham, nut, man

**Lesson 92**

*Phrases to be written*: a cat in sand, hut on a hill, nut in a hand

**Lesson 93**

*Missing parts*: cat's ears; hut on the hill; fish on the line; ant's dish

**Lesson 94**

| | |
|---|---|
| fin | lock |
| win | sock |
| nut | rock |
| hut | sack |
| sand | back |
| hand | shack |

**Lesson 95**

*Sequence of sentences*: it has a lid; he has a hat; she has a mitt.

**Lesson 96**

*Sentences to be circled*: she hears a cow; a man has ears; she got a rug; a man has a cat.

**Lesson 97**

Matching words should be circled.

**Lesson 98**

*Sentences to be written*: sam is sad; dan has a hut; the ram is fat; the sun is hot.

**Lesson 99**

*Missing parts*: man's hat, shack near lake, cat on gate, man that cow is licking

**Lesson 100**

| | |
|---|---|
| hate | kick |
| gate | sick |
| wish | lick |
| dish | sail |
| kiss | tail |
| miss | nail |

**Lesson 101**

*Sequence of sentences*: a rat is not fat; a ram is fat; a cat is fat.

**Lesson 102**

*k pictures*: kite, kiss, key, kick, king

**Lesson 103**

*Words to be circled*: fish, nail, dish, read, gate, seat

**Lesson 104**

| | | |
|---|---|---|
| fin | did | ham |
| man | rag | nut |
| hat | | |

**Lesson 105**

*Sentences to be written*: the man is old; the cow is fat; the hat was sold; the man is mad.

**Lesson 106**

*Missing parts*: fish in lake, ant on boy's nose, cake on plate, hats on shelf

**Lesson 107**

| | |
|---|---|
| sit | nut |
| hit | hut |
| sack | man |
| tack | can |
| tail | sock |
| mail | lock |

**Lesson 108**

*Words to be written*: cow, fan, hug, mom, hat, sun

**Lesson 109**

*(1)* no *(2)* yes *(3)* yes *(4)* yes
*(5)* no *(6)* no *(7)* no *(8)* yes
*(9)* yes

**Lesson 110**

| | | |
|---|---|---|
| win | sun | hug |
| nod | fan | wish |
| cow | | |

**Lesson 111**

*Sentences to be written*: mom is a cop; she has a dog; dan sits in sand; he digs for fun.

**Lesson 112**

*Sequence of words to be pasted on*: cats, sail, tail, ears, cake

**Lesson 113**

| | |
|---|---|
| hug | log |
| rug | dog |
| hot | goat |
| pot | coat |
| feed | seat |
| seed | meat |

**Lesson 114**

*Sentences to be circled*: she ate a fish; this dog is sad; kick the can; we have a goat.

**Lesson 115**

| | | |
|---|---|---|
| fun | lid | sun |
| mud | ran | hut |
| mom | | |

**Lesson 116**

*Sequence of sentences*: see the top go; see the ship go; see the dog go.

**Lesson 117**

*Missing parts*: car under kitten, ship's sail, cop's sock, girl holding goat

**Lesson 118**

*p pictures*: pan, pie, puppet, piano, pig, pumpkin, pillow, pipe, pencil

**Lesson 119**

| | |
|---|---|
| fish | kick |
| dish | lick |
| shave | sick |
| wave | mop |
| hug | cop |
| rug | top |

**Lesson 120**

*(1)* yes *(2)* yes *(3)* no *(4)* no
*(5)* yes *(6)* yes *(7)* no *(8)* yes
*(9)* yes

**Lesson 121**

*Sequence of words to be pasted on*: oats, game, read, little, far

**Lesson 122**

*(1)* cows *(2)* top *(3)* runs *(4)* nuts
*(5)* feet

**Lesson 123**

*ch pictures*: chair, church, cherries, chicks, chimney, cheese, chin, chain

**Lesson 124**

*Sentences to be written*: sal has a mop; she is with sam; I hug the cat; dan wins the mitt.

**Lesson 125**

*Sequence of words to be pasted on*: chips, nose, road, wet, lake

**Lesson 126**

*Words to be written*: hats, kitten, mop, dog, teeth, kiss

**Lesson 127**

*(1)* yes *(2)* yes *(3)* no *(4)* no
*(5)* yes *(6)* no *(7)* no *(8)* yes
*(9)* no

**Lesson 128**

*(1)* hut *(2)* hill *(3)* old *(4)* red

**Lesson 129**

*Phrases to be circled*: pet in bed, ten on can, men on ship

**Lesson 130**

*Sequence of sentences*: the pot is hot; the log is hot; the sun is hot.

**Lesson 131**

*b pictures*: bicycle, ball, bus, bone, bear, belt, butterfly, banana, bed, boots, bell

**Lesson 132**

*(1)* hats *(2)* digs *(3)* girl *(4)* lid
*(5)* hill

**Lesson 133**

*(1)* yes *(2)* yes *(3)* no *(4)* yes
*(5)* yes *(6)* no *(7)* yes *(8)* yes
*(9)* no

**Lesson 134**

*Words to be written*: sit, boy, ship, dig, sleep, corn

**Lesson 135**

*(1)* man *(2)* cat *(3)* bed *(4)* rug

**Lesson 136**

| | |
|---|---|
| arm | cow |
| teeth | fish |
| corn | feet |

**Lesson 137**

*Words to be written*: waving, bug, hill, car, pot, top

**Lesson 138**

*Phrases to be circled*: cops in corn, ram hugs sam, dish on fish

**Lesson 139**

*(1)* yes *(2)* no *(3)* yes *(4)* no
*(5)* yes *(6)* no

**Lesson 140**

*(1)* beds *(2)* red *(3)* hand *(4)* farms
*(5)* ponds

**Lesson 141**

*Words to be written*: pig, cow, rabbit, boy, girl, sheep

**Lesson 142**

*(1)* pigs *(2)* farm *(3)* mud *(4)* corn

**Lesson 143**

*Sequence of faces*: mean face, sad face, happy face, sick face

**Lesson 144**

*(1)* corn *(2)* frog *(3)* barn *(4)* rugs *(5)* wins

**Lesson 145**

*(1)* no *(2)* yes *(3)* yes *(4)* no *(5)* no

**Lesson 146**

*Sentences to be written*: a girl is digging; the boy is cold; he is her brother; they see a rabbit.

**Lesson 147**

| girl | pig |
|------|------|
| deer | dish |
| ship | brush |

**Lesson 148**

*(1)* man with paint can *(2)* dog with bone *(3)* girl with books *(4)* girl on crutches *(5)* boy with shopping cart

**Lesson 149**

*(1)* yes *(2)* no *(3)* no *(4)* yes *(5)* no *(6)* no *(7)* no *(8)* yes *(9)* yes

**Lesson 150**

*(1)* girl *(2)* brother *(3)* bus *(4)* park

**Lesson 151**

| red | log | box |
|-----|-----|-----|
| pig | cop | old |
| bug | | |

**Lesson 152**

*Sequence of faces*: angry face, tired face, sad face, happy face

**Lesson 153**

*Words to be written*: box, broom, moon, pool, fox, room

**Lesson 154**

*(1)* cars *(2)* dark *(3)* bugs *(4)* jumps *(5)* pets

**Lesson 155**

*(1)* digging *(2)* yard *(3)* dig *(4)* fun

**Lesson 156**

*(1)* girl with fishing pole *(2)* woman in bathing suit *(3)* person in space suit *(4)* boy with cat *(5)* cow

**Lesson 157**

*g pictures:* girl, goat, gate, garage, gum, guitar, ghost

**Lesson 158**

*(1)* no *(2)* yes *(3)* yes *(4)* no *(5)* yes

**Lesson 159**

*Words to be written*: well, swim, log, wet, hot, walk

**Lesson 160**

*Sequence of faces*: angry face, perspiring face, frightened face, smiling face

# Fast Cycle/Reading Mastery I
## Lesson Conversion Chart

*Fast Cycle I* is an accelerated version of *Reading Mastery I*. It is designed for students who need less repetition and drill than is provided in *Reading Mastery I*, and who can work at a faster pace.

Listed below are the *Fast Cycle/Reading Mastery I* lesson equivalents. Students at a particular lesson in the *Fast Cycle* program should be able to complete any of the worksheets in the equivalent *Reading Mastery I* lesson range.

| Fast Cycle Lesson | Reading Mastery I Lesson Range | Fast Cycle Lesson | Reading Mastery I Lesson Range | Fast Cycle Lesson | Reading Mastery I Lesson Range |
|---|---|---|---|---|---|
| 1 | 1-12 | 31 | 65-66 | 61 | 121-122 |
| 2 | 13-14 | 32 | 67 | 62 | 123-125 |
| 3 | 15-16 | 33 | 68-69 | 63 | 126 |
| 4 | 17-19 | 34 | 70-71 | 64 | 127-128 |
| 5 | 20-22 | 35 | 72-73 | 65 | 129-130 |
| 6 | 23 | 36 | 74-75 | 66 | 131-132 |
| 7 | 24-25 | 37 | 76 | 67 | 133-135 |
| 8 | 26 | 38 | 77-78 | 68 | 136-137 |
| 9 | 27 | 39 | 79-80 | 69 | 138 |
| 10 | 28-29 | 40 | 81-82 | 70 | 139-140 |
| 11 | 30-31 | 41 | 83-84 | 71 | 141-142 |
| 12 | 32-33 | 42 | 85-86 | 72 | 143-145 |
| 13 | 34-35 | 43 | 87-90 | 73 | 146 |
| 14 | 36 | 44 | 91 | 74 | 147 |
| 15 | 37-38 | 45 | 92-93 | 75 | 148-150 |
| 16 | 39 | 46 | 94 | 76 | 151-152 |
| 17 | 40-41 | 47 | 95-96 | 77 | 153-155 |
| 18 | 42 | 48 | 97-98 | 78 | 156 |
| 19 | 43-44 | 49 | 99-100 | 79 | 157 |
| 20 | 45 | 50 | 101-102 | 80 | 158 |
| 21 | 46-48 | 51 | 103-104 | | |
| 22 | 49-50 | 52 | 105 | | |
| 23 | 51 | 53 | 106 | | |
| 24 | 52-54 | 54 | 107-108 | | |
| 25 | 55-56 | 55 | 109-110 | | |
| 26 | 57-58 | 56 | 11-112 | | |
| 27 | 59-60 | 57 | 113-115 | | |
| 28 | 61 | 58 | 116 | | |
| 29 | 62-63 | 59 | 117-118 | | |
| 30 | 64 | 60 | 119-120 | | |